Hope you!

Jacqui

# Beyond the Surface

# Beyond
# the
# Surface

Jacquie Fazekas

**BEYOND THE SURFACE**

To those who are struggling to find their passion and purpose. May these writings inspire you to dive in and discover who you really are.

# Acknowledgements

I want to recognize my family and many friends who have encouraged me to discover my real self. They have loved me through both the dark and bright days of my life, never judging my decisions because they knew I owned them.

The deepest gratitude and recognition I must give to my mother, born into this world as Wendy Reina Cunningham. She never abandoned me, nor criticized me. She celebrated my uniqueness when I despised it. Since her death and transition from this world in 2014, she has been championing me from above. Without her never-ending love for me, I could not have discovered my true self and learned to see myself as God sees me.

# Contents

# Chronicling the Journey

Do you ever feel like you don't belong? Maybe you have felt lost and without hope or a sense of purpose. Perhaps you have experienced emotional pain that has been too much to bear some days.

I've been there, too.

Days can be long and lonely when you don't feel like you fit in or are so tired that you would rather stay in bed than face the world. Family and friends often do not know how to help because they do not seem to know themselves. Sometimes others try to fix us or offer advice that seems to be more self-serving for them than helpful for us.

Stress is said to be good, especially if you seem successful on the outside. But, stress eats away at the inner spirit. Many of us were taught to multi-task through life and were told it was a sign of success, but it just brings exhaustion. The negative and painful stress of juggling some of the most meaningful situations can drain us of whatever passion and energy for life that we have. Yet, we are conditioned to just keep going.

With every step, we become weaker and weaker until one day, we cannot go on. With confusion and exhaustion, we go seeking help and guidance. For some of us, it helps to self-medicate so the pain will go away. Other times it is medication to get us to sleep or help us cope throughout the day. For others, it might be ignoring or escaping the truth that is nagging inside. Most of us look to the outside world to make the pain go away or help us function from day to day.

Unfortunately, the day never really comes when we find full relief. We just keep chasing the quick fix. The only true solution to overcoming the deep pain and exhaustion is by facing the situations head on. All your fears, worries, confusion, and lack of fulfillment must be dealt with from the inside, not on the outside.

I know this because I was one of those highly successful people on the outside, but a mess on the inside. From my early childhood, I struggled to fit in. I was often sick with no good explanations. My parents divorced when I was a pre-teen and that sent me spiraling further into pain and suffering. I attempted to take control of my life during my teen years, chasing accolades from others and whatever promised pleasure. I lived to please others and to appear successful on the outside.

After three near-death experiences – the last one when I was 41 years old – I knew I had to do something to change my life's direction. I began to do the work necessary to discover my true self. I have been healing slowly. My reflections have caused me to search within, despite how painful it was at first. These reflections are the fruit of shedding old perspectives and gaining new ones on *my* life and on life in general.

None of us seek near-death experiences or anything else that can alter our lives and perspectives. Situations like that just happen to us. However, shifts in our lives – whether good or bad – are meant to move us upward toward greater fulfillment. How we choose to embrace these transitions determines whether we will experience from them gain or loss. I know that, like me, you desire gain in your life, not loss. So, with these reflections, I hope to help you get there.

I have always desired to live an inspiring and positive life. For the past several years, I have worked hard to maintain a growth mindset and look for opportunities that will better myself and others. Despite many failures, detours, and stumbles in my life, I can honestly say I treasure them all.

*Beyond the Surface* is a collection of my own reflections intended to stir thoughts and emotions inside of you that will help you discover – or rediscover – your true self. I hope they will also help you find some joy, hope, and a sense of purpose. As you take the time to read through these thoughts and reflect on the questions I've posed at the end of each chapter, my prayer is that you will discover not just who you are, but a more positive outlook on life, as well. It is also my prayer that throughout the pages of this book you will find your thoughts profoundly shifted and you'll be so inspired through the process that you'll share what you've learned with others. We can each make a difference in this world. This is my attempt. I can't wait to learn of yours.

# 1.

# A Story

You have a story that is unique and special.

It's a story that is longing to be told. It craves a voice and a listener. It has so many layers of feelings, experiences, drama, and pain that create a unique tale. Each moment of your life, another layer of wisdom and perspective can be added to your story, if you're ever aware of that story and focused on growing through your experiences. Your story ultimately paints a creative picture of your thoughts and feelings. One story is no better than the next; each has purpose and a teaching threaded through it.

Did you know that darkness and light exists in every story? It is with these contrasting elements that you and I can better understand our *entire* story. Sharing only part of a story serves to mislead and disguise the truth. You and I can tend to only tell parts of our stories to others – and even to ourselves – to avoid criticism and pain. Yet our complete stories are full of precious life lessons for those who are willing to listen.

Each person's story is deep and mysterious. It can have off-shoots of comedy and laughter. No doubt, the only way to tell a story is to relay thoughts from the heart that exude love. It takes a lot of courage to expose all the interesting crevices of each of our stories. But as you tell the whole truth, the raw and painful moments that you fear might make people reject you actually have a way of drawing in the listener. And your joyful moments can offer hope to others.

Our stories are not written in one day; only paragraphs, chapters, or perhaps just a sentence are. A story is dreamt up first in the Writer's mind. Through every thought, feeling, and action, the words are created and the story begins. The twists and turns in the storyline are evidence that the Creator's inspirations and choices flow through us to craft the story. The Writer owns where our story begins and ends. A story could take a lifetime to write. Do you realize Someone is writing your story?[1] And that story is still being lived out by you…and waiting to be told to others.

---

[1] Psalm 139:16 says "You [God] saw me before I was born. Every day of my life was recorded in your book. Every moment was laid out before a single day had passed."

Short stories with lots of impact can have a very purposeful lesson. A lengthy story with very little impact on the listener has a different result. Nevertheless, it is still a story waiting to be heard. Poetic stories are joyful and amazing, with the artful depictions unbelievably connected. Dramas are some of the most prevalent and enjoyed storylines. In them, there is so much material to be written about that the book virtually writes itself!

## Everyone Has a Story

Every person desires to have a voice and be heard. Being heard is just the start; for each story really needs to be listened to attentively so someone understands the plot and outcome. A story trapped inside of us, is a wasted lesson in life. Stories teach us about ourselves, and those around us about themselves. Sometimes our stories make the listener uncomfortable, but every story evokes feelings. Feelings stirred from the inside cause us to connect with others. A story always has a purpose.

I woke up in 2015 with a strong desire to tell my story, but really only had a few parts that I could remember. My childhood was a blank slate. I could remember only fragments of life and began to wonder what I had buried so deep in order to forget. For about a year, I asked my family about their experiences with me when I remembered some storylines that helped me fill in the blanks. I soon realized that I would need to do the hard work of going really deep inside my subconscious to confront my fears, doubts, and worries. I would have to question everything I believed about myself and ask why I felt the way I did. I knew if I was going to rediscover my story, I would have to be okay with exposing every feeling inside of me. It was not going to be an easy process, but I had been numb for so long, that I just craved to really know myself – my true story. Something deep within was calling me.

With each day that I continued to ask questions and continued that process within, I rediscovered a new piece of myself. Soon, I became obsessed with asking others their stories because I knew how good it felt to start sharing mine.

## It's Your Turn

Try asking another person about his or her story. When you ask with a genuine curiosity, and with a caring and loving spirit, you may draw out someone else's story. It might be a story that will inevitably change your perspective, deepen your understanding, embed empathy, or cause greater feelings of compassion. If you actively listen for the layers of truth, pain, joy, and the churning of many feelings, you will be drawn in and soon feel you're a part of the story, too. Your own story may shift. It is still your story, but it's been impacted by another storyline.

With a loving heart, try asking a homeless man what his story is. What you believed to be the storyline will be exposed as truth or fiction. Too often, we end up creating a fictitious story from our own story. Fictitious storylines do not serve any purpose but to deceive others. A true story makes a connection with the listener.

In an open, non-judgmental manner, ask an older person whom you know and respect to tell you his or her story. You may hear a life story full of wisdom and inspiration. Depending on who you ask and what their story is, you may be changed and experience stirring emotions you have not felt in a while. Tears, laughter, pain, heartache, and much more will draw you in.

Try taking the time to listen to the story of a young teenager. As we get older, we tend to project our own reality onto others. More often than not, we discover a much deeper truth in another person's story.

Asking and listening are the key components in building a bridge of connection with someone else. Our own story becomes less interesting and less impactful when kept inside. It serves no one, not even ourselves. It is one of so many paradoxes in life – self-serving behaviors are really self-sabotaging. Thus, listening to our own story does not grow us. We must understand and listen to others' stories to grow and make connections.

A story serves to grow those who listen to it. When a story is heard, the author is then affirmed and validated. Each of us is an author of sorts of our own life (in that we have choices that God gives us), as well as a listener. The natural engagement of being both should illuminate the desire in each of us to connect more meaningfully with others. By authentically sharing a story and actively listening to a story, it is a fluid dance of energy between two people.

A story is written over a lifetime, but it is also written during moments. Perhaps you will find yourself a character in another person's story. What role will you play? Have you ever thought about the impact you have on a story? Your attitudes and actions in life affect others' storylines. Do you realize you are a part of other people's stories? How do you want to define your character? Would you listen to another person's story with greater attentiveness if you thought you were in it? When you think about it, our character shows up in our own story but might show up differently in someone else's.

Truly, your story and mine is simply a chapter or verse in the greater book called "life." We are bound together as one story, a bigger story, by the pages of our lives. The characters, ebbing and flowing from one chapter to the next, have quite a lot in common. We are all in one story under heaven…and we all have choices in how we want that story to play out.

The collective book of "life" never really finishes being written because new stories are always being added to it.

### *Every one of us has a story to tell and to be heard.*

What part of your story are you longing to tell?


Who do you want to share it with?


What is hindering you from telling your stories?

"There is no greater agony than bearing an untold story inside you."

--Maya Angelou

# 2.

# Carefree

Swing from the trees, play in the dirt, swim in the pool, and learn to live carefree. You and I were born without concerns. We laughed without instruction, smiled from the inside out, and never thought about the need to have control over anything.

As we grew older, we drifted further into ego living, feeling like we were stronger, knew more, and could control our lives better. We sought to maintain control in order to avoid pain, conflict, uncertainty. Today, the more we learn and think we know, the stronger our will and ego becomes. Alas, ego demands control!

It took me a long time to realize this. As a single mom of two boys, I had a busy executive corporate job and I believed I was in control. In fact, I would call myself a "control freak" as if that was an honor. The more I showed I was in control, the more my ego was controlling me. I became consumed with power, success, status, and what other people thought of me. If I showed any weakness at all, I was not in control.

When I was 41 years old and living my "dream life" I was struck down with a seizure and cardiac arrest while travelling for work. *Who was really in control then?* I quickly realized that I was not and that God had enough of me not listening to Him and trying to control everything. There had been plenty of signs and messages to slow down, but I did not listen. At this stage in my life, my two sons were busy preteens with lots of demands on me personally. Plus, I had just been elevated to Vice President at my company – a position I had worked hard to attain my entire career. Sometimes it takes this type of life jolt to really wake us up to focus on the important things and not the superficial ones. I learned quickly that I needed to release control and follow God more intently than I had been doing.

You and I can release control, let go of our egos, and start to live carefree!

How? Surrender control to God's plan for your life – and not your own – and experience the peace that comes from trusting the Only One who really is in control. With the positive energy that flows forward when you and I surrender control, we can begin moving toward the release of our ego.

Our frustration at trying to control our circumstances is God's way of reminding us that *He* is in control. Swimming against the positive energy current is draining. It is the paradox of life; the more control we think we have, the less we really have. No wonder so many souls feel empty. Once I was able to release control, I learned to live carefree.

Perhaps you are trying to control something now and it's only causing you frustration and pain. Trust God that He knows the plan and that He has us flowing in a positive direction despite the turbulent waves![2] Giving up control does not mean you do nothing and wait. It simply means you pay attention to God's voice to help guide you.

### *Trust and release control!*

What area of control are you having a hard time releasing?

What is difficult in your life at this time? Could it be that you are trying to control the outcome?

What is the worst thing that could happen if you gave up control to God?

---

[2] Romans 8:28 tells us "And we know that God causes everything to work together for the good of those who love God and are called according to his purpose for them."

# 3.
# Self-Discovery

Discovering one's true self can be a process that is both difficult and scary. We look around to the outside world for the answers and for someone to blame. The inside world is often neglected or shut out completely. With pain and yearning for more knowledge of ourselves, we focus on stopping both the pain and the yearning. It is easy to silence or numb ourselves into a complacent routine that we are comfortable with, just to avoid self-discovery.

Finding out who we are and what makes us tick can be a painful process. Therefore, it is only when the pain from the outside is so strong that we go within to discover more, because there is no other place to turn. It is when our curiosity about ourselves is so deep that we must sit quietly to discover the answers to our most yearning questions about ourselves.

Self-discovery is worth the painful process. It is a freeing experience that sheds the mind chains, and fades the fears and self-doubt that we carry around. It unlocks confusion and gives clarity and answers to the deep questions we have been asking.

For only when you go deep within can the truth of self be discovered. Then the soul smiles with joy and peace as it is no longer trapped and hidden from one's thoughts.

Empowerment, strength, and happiness come from knowing the inner sanctuary of your true self. Life is all about the journey and is definitely more fulfilling when you add self-discovery to the roster of adventures! You can then be authentically yourself without the desire for anything more.

### Don't be afraid of self-discovery.

What do you long to discover about yourself?

Are you willing to do what it takes to discover yourself? Even if it is painful?


What will you do differently today to discover who you really are?

# 4.

# Broken Is Beautiful

We have been conditioned to avoid the idea of being weak or broken. We are told from an early age not to show weakness, that we must be strong.

Admit it. You've heard people say, "Hide your feelings because if you show your feelings you are vulnerable." Yet, vulnerability, authenticity, and being real with ourselves is the only way to build a strong foundation of love and meaningful connections with others.

Broken is beautiful because it reveals your truest self to the world and celebrates that perfection is just an illusion – the masks we choose to wear for the outer world. Unfortunately, our inner self knows that it is a mask. As we wear a mask to hide fear, pain, and insecurity, we have a difficult time connecting with others in an authentic way. It is an "imagined reality" built on denial and fictitious emotions. Can you see this paradox? The brokenness that we hide from is the very thing that creates our wholeness.

Eventually, the mask becomes worn and old, then the true being behind the mask must be revealed. Why must we wait until we are old and worn out to reveal the truth of ourselves? We need to comfort each other by making brokenness a normal phenomenon. In fact, brokenness is normal, it's the acceptance and acknowledgement of it that is rare. When we realize that we are all broken[3] and that acknowledgement of our brokenness is the first step to God making us beautiful, we will truly understand how resilient and strong we are. Being able to admit we are broken is the journey to purpose. When we are broken, we can also connect with others in a real way.

I had to go deep within my own thoughts and feelings to discover the lies I was telling myself. I realized that so much of what I was holding up as true success was simply just the mask of success. When I went deep – by asking myself some hard questions and facing truths about myself that were hard to accept – I started to peel off the masks I had worn for years. It was painful to look at those masks straight-on and give witness to the lies. No one really knew the lies I was living; they saw the lies as my truth. As I began to accept my brokenness, I began to heal. By

---

[3] Romans 3:23 says "All of us have sinned and fallen short of God's glory."

accepting that I was broken, I was able to invite God to shine into those broken places and rebuild my true self. My connections to my family and friends became deeper and more meaningful. As a result, my family and friends started to open up more authentically, too. In my professional life, I started to stand up for myself and create healthy boundaries.

God breaks us down to build us up! Why would we not celebrate that journey? The Apostle Paul, who wrote much of the New Testament, said he used to consider his achievements as his strengths but upon realizing what God could do through his brokenness, he said "I will boast only about my weaknesses" (2 Corinthians 12:5). One of his life lessons was realizing that when he was weak, he was strong.[4] God will only rebuild those who allow themselves to be broken. And He can make us better and stronger than before. What a gift!

**The strength to rebuild your brokenness into a beautiful soul requires getting REAL!**

What do you need to get REAL about in your life?

What do you fear is stopping you from admitting you are broken and in need of being rebuilt?

If you got real with yourself, what would crumble? And what could God rebuild that into? Dream a little.

---

[4] In 2 Corinthians 12:8-10, Paul said "Three different times I begged the Lord to take it (his debilitating weakness) away. Each time [God] said, "My grace is all you need. My power works best in weakness." So now I am glad to boast about my weaknesses, so that the power of Christ can work through me…. For when I am weak, then I am strong."

# 5.

# Because

I have this thing about wanting everything to be explained.

Apparently, I was born curious. I was born with a "why" switch. It took me many years to realize that not everything has an explanation. Even for myself, I felt compelled to have to explain everything to everyone. I longed to know how things work, why they work, and the best way to get something done. Do you do that, too? Put everything through your mind's lens to compartmentalize and make sense of all the data and input coming at you every moment? *Why?*

Just like a computer overloads and freezes, so do we. We know there is a reason behind the computer freeze because we have been taught there *must* be a reason. When it unfreezes, we explain it away as a technical problem and simply move on without trying to offer a thorough explanation. Yet, we choose to believe there was a reason.

Just like with our laptops and devices, when we overload and freeze up and become stuck in life, we immediately look for the reason. We become restless trying to get unstuck and sometimes hit the buttons that are not meant to be hit. This leads to further problems and more freeze-ups. Our natural impatient hardwiring always wants an explanation and "just because" is not good enough. We look to the world around us to provide explanations, excuses or something or someone to blame.

### There must be a "because"

You and I cannot compartmentalize our existence without a "because." It cannot get filed in our mind correctly without a reason. Sometimes being stuck just means that our "freeze time" needs to be longer. We must learn to rest without impatience.

What if you and I learned to be okay without having to understand it all? We are not machines, but beautiful complex purposeful beings. God works on us – and our wiring – moment by moment when we allow Him to do the necessary work. Yet sometimes, in order for Him to do His work on us, He must slow us down and literally freeze us at a point. Again, it is not our natural tendency to freeze, or to even be okay with a freeze, but when it happens we should realize that there are some serious things being worked on behind the scenes on our wiring so we can get unstuck.

When we experience a freeze-up, it is not the time to start hitting the wrong buttons and getting impatient with our "freeze time". It just causes more issues. Be patient, let God do the work and watch. Sometimes He'll do that work through others around us – through some advice we needed to hear, or a situation that frustrates us and makes us experience a time-out. Seek to understand, but don't look for the "because." Give it time. Give *God* time – to work in *you*.

Often the "because" becomes apparent in the freeze and is the very answer and explanation that unfreezes you into action.

Be okay with saying, "just because," instead of worrying about knowing! If I can do it, you can, too. God asks us to trust and believe. Hebrews 11:6 says "Without faith, it is impossible to please God." If we always need a "because" we are not relinquishing control to Him.

The best moments of discovery and celebration in my life have come from the unexpected and the unexplained. It can work that way in your life, too. There is often not an obvious explanation for the result. The "because" is driven by God and needs no explanation.

Celebrate and relish in the joy of the "because" -- because He loves you![5]

**Experience peace in the fact that God knows the 'because" and we don't have to.**

Think about it. Why do you feel you need a "because"?

Can you trust that God has a plan without having to understand why?

What can you do to be more comfortable with not knowing?

---

[5] John 3:16

# 6.
# Ask "Why?"

Do you ask why or just proceed with judgment?

How often do you notice you have jumped to a conclusion and then after you hear more of the story, you realize you should have stopped to ask more "whys?"

Why do people walk down the street on a beautiful fall day and look miserable? Are they even aware of the message their body language is communicating? What is going on in their lives? Why do people never stop to talk to the homeless? Are they afraid to lose everything they have? Why do some people get frustrated in every moment? Have they ever known joy in their lives? What are we afraid of?

As I was walking in the city one day, what I observed revealed a lot about the world we live in. Fast-paced, self-centered, distracted, grumpy people filled the sidewalks. I thought to myself, *How much faster can our world get?*

Beyond fast, we want everything to be instantaneous. To us, instant must be better than fast, and fast better than slow. Outward and instant answers and fixes are our chief cravings. Instant food, instant results, instant love; the list is endless.

Can you relate?

One of the paradoxes in life is that the faster we go, the slower and lesser our lives become. With less sleep, less healthy food, less communication, less dreams, less laughter, less trust... must I go on? My life was fast and definitely not fulfilled. I began to ask myself "why" concerning my habits, beliefs, and fears because I was seeking something deeper than I had. With that one word, I slowed my entire fabricated reality down to discover the truth and the misinterpreted reality that my mind had tricked me into believing. It slowed my emotions down, to enable me to begin to care and love more.

After that day of being more present in the moment, I could see the value in asking "why?" It became a passion of mine to ask "why" at the oddest times, about the oddest things, and with most everyone I would meet. Cultivating a curious mind enables you to go deeper within and also connect deeper with others.

Why do raw foods give us the answer to understand, slow down, and enjoy nature's bounty? Asking "why" stimulates all six senses in us and awakens the truth in us. It creates an emotional connection between us and others. Slowing down is not tantamount to being lazy or weak. Rather, it is a powerful awakening that moves us so much faster to the truth and our fulfillment!

### *Don't be afraid to ask "why?"*

What have you always wondered about, but never stopped to ask "why?"

Do you find yourself asking "why" about certain attitudes, beliefs and behaviors of yours? If so, what are they? If not, why not?

How can you encourage others to ask "why?"

# 7.
# Be Mindful

At one time, I wasn't nearly as mindful about my thoughts and actions. I did not make the connection that my thoughts were determining my actions and thus determining my outcomes. The outcomes in my life were not always positive and growth minded. I'm so glad now that I learned that lesson.

Be mindful of your thoughts. They determine your life path. Course-correct your thoughts daily. Break free of the judgmental thoughts, not good-enough thoughts, *why them and not me?* thoughts. Being mindful means having a mind that is fulfilled. Being "mind-fulfilled."

How we perceive people, space, and time is purely based on our mindfulness. Change your mind, change your world.

I know what you're thinking. *That's easier said than done.* You're right.

It is natural to think critically and judgmentally. It is not natural to be calm when you want to be angry. Life hands us moments, and gives us practice daily to be mindful of our thoughts and attitudes. *Attitude is everything!*

### Practicing Mindfulness

This concept of choosing your attitude was something I would emphasize to my children regularly, but I did not always walk the talk. With the busy days, pressures from work and personal life, being tired with very little time for what was important to me, I neglected to be mindful of my attitude. Life has us all going full speed through our day and barely breathing along the way. It is our choice to slow down or accept that crazy pace of life. Our attitude is always our choice. No one else can choose it for us.

Mindfulness is a choice, too. It is a moment in time that makes you slow down and think. Every day is full of moments that eventually make the day. Each moment is a chance to be mindful of our thoughts and actions. When you have negative vibes and thoughts, thinking of the opposite helps! Think of the positive, be without judgment, and live in the space of love. Mindful love is powerful!

Life takes on positive energy when love is the driver in the quest to be good, to be loved, and to see the potential in others.

*Be mindful and start noticing life around you.*

How do you control and choose your attitude?

In what areas of your life can you be more mindful?

In what way can you alter your attitude in order to bring    about positive change?

# 8.
# Be the Light

What does it mean to be the light?
   I use to hear this phrase pretty regularly in church, in my friend circles, and I'd even read it in quotes over social media. I would think to myself, Easier said than done!

One day, when I was in deep reflection, I heard this explanation:

"Amongst the dark clouds, be the sunshine that refuses to be dimmed by the clouds, irrespective of the negativities around.
"Be the positivity that is heard in the silence. Be the smile that says so much, but yet makes no sound. Be the love that makes the heart beat faster and empowers the breath, not takes it away. Be the crazy energy that invigorates the soul and yet calms the thoughts.
"Be the smell of sweetness, not the smell of decay. Be the light, a small but mighty particle of Me."

This message had a profound effect on me and thrust me into a much deeper appreciation for simply enjoying moments. It caused me to be more present and loving toward others. With each day since I heard His voice, I practice being "the light" – whether it involves being the optimist in the room, bringing the humor to a situation, or speaking an encouraging word to someone who needs it.

### *Light up the darkness around you.*

What do you find difficult about being "the light" for someone else?

Who can you start being "the light" for today?




Who has lit the way in your darkness?

# 9.

# Blessings

There are blessings in each moment we breathe.

Do you see them in your own life? How do you count so many blessings?

I would suggest you don't keep score, but relish in deep gratitude for each blessing you encounter. With every dusk, say "thank you" to God.

I have learned that blessings come in the form of both pain and pleasure. I used to only give thanks for the good things, until the day I started reflecting deeply about my life. I began to see the connections between the painful moments and the positive growth I experienced from it. It was a revelation to me that painful moments could be positive, thus they were blessings, too. After that awakening, things shifted in my perspective and how I dealt with painful situations. I have started to embrace these times, rather than fear them. I realized that blessings propel us to grow and consistently change. It is important we express gratitude over grief, pain, pleasure, and joy, because our attitude really matters.

Embrace each one of life's blessings and go with the flow. Wish for something purposeful and blessings will come. It might not come in the form that you hoped, but trust that God knows best. Having genuine trust, faith, hope, and love, summon the blessing moments!

*Blessings come in the form of both pain and pleasure.*

What significant blessings have you experienced?

What painful moments are you now realizing were blessings?

How will you practice seeing and appreciating the small   blessings every day?

"It is during our darkest moments that we must focus to see the light."

--Aristotle

# 10.
# Broken for a Purpose

My Dear One,

I have broken you down and I know it hurts. I know you do not understand the reason, but it is for a purpose. Unless you are in pieces, I cannot rebuild you into a more beautiful being than you were before. You wandered from Me and daily worked on destroying yourself, your beauty, and your soul. I let you make choices throughout your life, hoping that you would openly choose good over the temptations and distractions of your ego. But you didn't. Before it was too late, I needed to step in and break you of those wrong choices and behaviors.

You are magnificent,[6] for I created you, but it is important than you feel it! I will guide you through rebuilding yourself into an even greater magnificent soul than you had thought possible. I have witnessed daily your strength, your determination and your passion. I can see that you have so much to give the world. As you rebuild yourself, you will see your worth in My eyes and understand all you are capable of. You will honor yourself – because you belong to Me – and soon feel the great purpose I have for you.

Being broken into pieces allows you to discover every part of yourself that I created. You are complex and magnificent! That is why everyone is unique! Please relish in being broken in this moment, feel My presence and guidance. You are being broken for a purpose!

Love,
Your Creator.

If you get quiet and reflective with your Maker you may begin to hear what He has been wanting to say to you.

---

[6] Ephesians 2:10 says "For we are God's masterpiece. He has created us anew in Christ Jesus, so we can do the good things he planned for us long ago."

*Embrace your brokenness, for it has a purpose.*

Are you feeling broken? In what way?

At what time in your life did you feel most broken? Can you connect the dots as to why He broke you into pieces?

What is the purpose He might have for rebuilding you?

# 11.
# Chaos

Chaos!
It is a powerful word that defines so much of our lives, and to some degree, how we have shifted in our lifestyle. We have allowed ourselves to be programmed to be dissatisfied with everything we have, so we can pursue something our culture says is better. Never being satisfied or happy with our today amounts to chaos. Worry and anxiety across all age groups is off the charts. This is chaos in our minds. Chasing the clock and saying there is not enough hours in a day -- chaos!

Efficiency with technology keeps our expectations higher, keeps us running out of hours, and keeps us disconnected from others, except through our devices - chaos!

Nature does not judge. Nature does not race the clock to grow or stay hardwired with technology. Nature is at peace with "now" and it is why our spirits seek nature so often when chaos is too much to handle.

Why do we choose chaos over peace? I'll tell you why. We are tempted by our egos to want more than we deserve. We start to believe that we are deserving. Our egos take over our thoughts and intentions and make us believe that we are entitled. This causes chaos! We are not more important than Him. Chaos is created by believing we are greater and more important than God.

For much of my adult years, I felt my life was full of chaos and it was! I was running on over-drive in nearly every area. I had no time to appreciate anything, not even my most precious gift – my two sons. I was multi-tasking every moment, and the result was that I was never fully present for anything.

One day, I woke up to this glaring reality. I was in the middle of chasing a bigger and better job. It was going to take another move. At the time, I was preparing for my oldest son to go into his first year of college and my second son was going into his senior year of high school. After prayers flowing out to God one night as I fell asleep, I was jolted awake with His voice telling me:

"You never get the moments back. You must learn to live NOW and be present. There will never be another first-year college football game, there will never be another senior year of high school, and you will never get these times back with your kids. There will always be another job. Experience life, stop running from it! Live in the moment, not in the future."

That was my awakening in 2015.

Conquer ego, avoid chaos, live in the NOW. The "More Factor" – more, more and more – will only lead to Chaos.  The "NOW Factor" is the peaceful path!

### Be present now!

What are you chasing that is leading to chaos?

Do you find you desire more stuff and more status over more meaningful moments?

Is the idea of "living in the moment" painful to you? If so, why?

# 12.
# Live Naturally

L ive as naturally as you can.
     Be as gentle as a butterfly and as patient as a snail. Be as flexible as a piece of grass and as strong as an old tree. Be as vibrant as a rose and as calm as a pond. Be as fluid as the water and as light as the sun.

In your dark times, may you find the peacefulness in the moon, for it lives in darkness, but gives hope with the dim light. In the grey fog, cherish the nourishment from the mist -- it cleanses.

As I started to begin to live in the moment, I began to look at nature differently. I would see lessons from nature with every turn.

It is quite amazing the creativity you find in nature. For who could have imagined a rainbow? It gives a joyous perspective of a journey from one point to the other. Sunsets change with every evening. They are colorful in their own right and never apologize for being different each day. To the mind's eye they are different,  yet they are still sunsets Nothing from the core changed, just the expression to the world, based on the environment around it.

God has provided all that we need to fulfill our purpose and He has given us examples in nature. Nature has obeyed His guidance. Nature exists and serves. It does not take or conquer.

I believe that it is God's desire for you and me to slow down and notice nature around us.

Let's open our eyes each day and see nature's examples of how we can live more simply and at peace. We are blessed in each moment to be able to breathe, flow, and exist. Let us learn to live as gently as nature lives, and to serve as nature serves.

***Love, learn, and live naturally.***

At what times during the day can you slow down to appreciate nature?

What parts of nature do you find yourself frustrated with? How can you look at the positive aspects of it?

What are your favorite elements of nature?

# 13.
# A Prayer for Purpose

Dear God,
        May I awaken each morning with awestruck amazement at this beautiful world You created. The sky shifts through a tapestry of color until it shines bright and celebrates the day ahead. My dreams have been small for myself, so I surrender to You, for I cannot compete with the dreams You have for me.

I want to live on purpose with every moment and every breath, in the same way that nature is on purpose! Your creations are purposeful and I stare in wonder at it all. I am one of Your creations, thus I know I was created with a purpose!

I want to live it out fully. I shed the fear, the worry, and the attempt to control and direct my purpose. I leave it with You. I am grateful for life! And so very grateful for my purpose.

May I always be on purpose with each wink, smile, sound of my voice, and movement in my body. May my thoughts and emotions be guided by You to fulfill the role You have for me on this earth!

With gratitude,
Your loving servant

I wrote that prayer at a time in my life when I had just faced a job transition. I knew God was moving me out of corporate life, but I was unsure of the next move. I shared this prayer humbly with you, so that you might be inspired to write your own. Go ahead and give it a try. He would love to hear what you have to say.

*Live each day on purpose.*

Do you know the purpose He has for you?

How can you live intentionally, every day, on purpose?




What do you need to commit to God in order to live on purpose?

# 14.

# Feelings

Feelings help you examine your past, present and future.

They are often met with resistance due to the pain. A resistant mindset refusing to acknowledge the presence of feelings creates a strong pull and push of emotions. Feelings often side-swipe you and jolt you, while bringing you into a significant awakening, causing you to be forever transformed.

*The presence of feelings is the only way to feel alive!*

Feelings are not just emotions on the surface, but a melted combination of all of our senses into one gigantic masterpiece! For instance, feeling love is created with warmth of touch, sight, sound, taste, smell, and energy vibrations.

I discover all my feelings during my self-discovery process. Some of them I had buried deep inside myself. I thought they were dead, but they were calling me from my belly every day. It is that stirring feeling, that uncomfortable space we want to avoid, but cannot. In the process of releasing all my feelings into the open, I began to recognize that they all served a purpose. It was in my acceptance of the negative feelings, that I could begin to develop a deeper understanding of myself, my past, and the fears that were holding me back from a great future.

Life is a tapestry of feelings that make us fully alive. Love is the most powerful feeling that overcomes every other emotion. Feelings aren't good or bad, in themselves. They are yours and make up who you are. That is why feeling so deeply is the biggest gift you can give yourself.

*All feelings need to be cherished in the moment!*

It is not enough to feel on the surface through one sense. Feelings cannot be fully comprehended without the depth of all senses. Knowing how good the self-discovery process is, I encourage you to unearth your feelings that might be hidden deep inside. Peel back the layers of disgust and shame and let those feelings breathe. Experience them all fully. Taste, smell, touch, hear, see, and FEEL…the sixth sense!

### *Feel and awaken all of you!*

What are you feeling in this moment?

What emotions are you afraid to feel?

What is the worst thing that could happen if you released all of your buried feelings? What is the best thing that could happen?

# 15.
# Let Me Fall

I must fall.

I cried out to God, "Please do not rescue me. I learn with every stumble and I treasure my growth through the hardship. I know it is not a common perspective, but I am not common. I am a person focused on growth. I have recognized that with some situations, I must fall hard in order to regain my strength!"

I do not look at failure as a brick wall that prevents us from moving forward. Rather, I see it as a learning platform to elevate one's understanding in the moment. This is a treasure, not a burden. Frankly, I run toward failure and relish my learnings and struggles. I know that with every struggle a portal of growth in life exists. Do you run to or from failure?

I believe failure can be a treasure. For with every failure, I am closer to my truer self! Some people might call their failures stepping stones, but not obvious ones. Sometimes the waves of fear and doubt obscure the visibility of those stones. One step, one failure, one recovery, one learning; such a beautiful amazing journey.

So there I sat in the river's flow, crying for help, knowing I must fall. The river of self-doubt, and fear of failure and not being good enough swirled around me as I quivered with chills. I wanted to be rescued from the pain, but I knew that the pain would rescue me eventually to a greater self within.

I know that hope lies in the struggle, but I did not like it! "Who cares?" God seems to shout out to me! "You need to learn that your struggles are your greatest gifts and you must struggle in order to fulfill your purpose. You have great work to be done here. I can rescue you, but for your own growth and maturity, you must fall."

Crumbled under my tears, I yelled "Let me fall! I know I have purposeful work here that I need to complete before I die. Don't rescue me!"

Then, I heard God's loud forceful voice, "Turn to Me and you will find true strength and resilience. What you thought was good for you was only your deceptive ego-self tempting you. When will you wake up to this truth? When will you recognize the deceptive self, versus your true self?"

Perhaps this time!" I cried out loud. Still not really knowing the strong hold of this world, I cried out to God one last time, "Let me fall!"

Life's greatest joys are experienced through overcoming struggles. We are then able to serve others by imparting our wisdom and sharing empathy about the struggles we've experienced. Failures are meant to break down our confidence in ourselves. Too often we have fictitious ideas of who we are.

### *Don't be afraid to fall.*

At what time in your life did you pray to be rescued from pain?

How do you look at failure in your life?

Do you listen and obey God when He urges you to trust Him?

# 16.

# Gifts Create

What do gifts create?
They create love, thoughtfulness, caring, passion, energy, joy, blessings, and life. Gifts can be cold, thoughtless, and useless too. We must realize the message we convey when offering gifts to one another.

Gifts create emotions without knowing. Physical gifts are outward manifestations and transfer of feelings from one person to another. Often gifts are physical actions that we do for others. They tell the world what we believe in, what we value, and what we think.

This idea that "gifts create" came to me over the holidays when I witnessed the various emotions from others as they were giving and receiving gifts. Sometimes, the gifts were not well received and I could tell were viewed as thoughtless and worthless, despite the monetary value of them. Other gifts were small. They were much more worthless in stature, but significantly more meaningful and valuable to the receiver.

Have you ever felt like another person simply did not care about you when they gave you a physical gift? On the other hand, have you felt the immense value of someone giving you the gift of their time?

The most precious gifts that last a lifetime are those moments and memories we make with others.

Reflect on the value of a handwritten card, scribbled on paper, that a child gives to his parents. Or the thought behind the husband's gift of a box of chocolates to his wife who wants to lose weight. What would you feel if you were to receive such gifts?

*Gifts create.*

Goodwill, love, passion, a sense of obligation, resentment, boredom. How the feelings swirl around in our minds when we give or receive a gift.

Gifts can also be shared with a lot more people than we realize. We can each share our personal gifts and talents with the world at large. Gifts come in all forms and are given and received throughout our lives. They create our reality and our relationships. I look at the act of giving very differently now, realizing I need to be more intentional and thoughtful when I give and receive.

### *Discover your gifts -- give wisely, and share wisely!*

What gifts should you be sharing with the world?

What gifts has God given you? How did they make you feel?

What gifts to you remember the most from childhood? Which one meant the most to you?

# 17.

# Go Slow, Go Fast

To go slow, yet to go fast. How paradoxical is that?
It is only when we look deeper into that which is obvious, that we discover the paradoxes of life; the real truth.

In order for us to accomplish more in the hustle and bustle of our daily lives, we must go slower than expected. We must slow our mind down to really understand a situation and its consequences. To slow down is uncomfortable for many and viewed as lazy by most.

It is in slowing down that we make less mistakes. We care more and are more calculated in our feelings, thinking, and actions. By slowing down, we are more deliberate and therefore can be more intentional in our pace at which we accomplish.

How quickly are you moving these days?

I was always going fast, until I realized that it was actually slowing me down. At work, when I would move quickly, I would forget to include key people in a meeting, thus jeopardizing a relationship. In my personal life, I would not foster meaningful connections with friends because I never had the time to do so.

"Go slow to go fast" is just one of many paradoxes in life. Go slow to train your mind to be curious about other paradoxes and to absorb the life messages they hold. For example, living in the light might mean we are in our darkest moments, and living in darkness is where we are able to detect the power of light. In silence and stillness, we learn actively what we are seeking to understand. Yet, in the busyness of conversations and movements, understanding often eludes us and leaves us confused.

It is a powerful awakening to begin to detect the paradoxes of life and live in the opposite of the expected.

*Paradoxes can empower the soul to freedom and accomplishments.*

What are a few paradoxes of life that you can think of?

Can you recall in your own life when going fast has hindered your progress?

What areas of your life do you think would benefit from slowing down?

# 18.
# Hidden Strength

Despite our physical state, we each have a hidden strength.

Our hidden strength is what we need to rely on in moments of weakness. For some of us, our hidden strength is God. We might feel weak in spirit, but God is always ready to fight for those who are His.[7] When your heart is pounding and your mind is racing, trust in your hidden strength.

I discovered my hidden strength while I was working my way out of an emotionally abusive marriage. No one could understand why I had put up with it for so long, but I knew I had some lessons to learn. Sometimes it takes a while for God to reveal the lessons and for us to learn them.

I learned that I must have stronger boundaries in order to let myself be loved in a healthy way. I discovered I was stronger and more resilient than I thought. I was able to heal by loving and forgiving my ex-husband. It was easy to do when I realized the lessons I had learned from some tumultuous years with him.

Our hidden strength is waiting for each of us. Tap into your hidden strength by loving daily. You will shift your world and that of others!

***We can choose to grow through anything God allows to come our way.***

How can you tap into your hidden strength daily?

Will you deploy love as a way to combat negativity?

How can you encourage others to reach for their hidden strengths?

---

[7] The Bible says "If God is for us, who can ever be against us" (Romans 8:31).

"You must live in the present,
launch yourself on every wave,
find your eternity in each moment."

-- Henry David Thoreau

# 19.
# Curiosity

How do we stay curious, joyous, and adventurous as we grow from an infant into an adult?

An infant only knows that he or she is loved and sees everything as new. The sights, sounds, textures, and smells all beckon the mind to wander and be adventurous. As the days, months and years get added to our age, we slowly grow less curious and wander further from our adventurous life.

Curiosity is a powerful feeling. It propels learning, growth, adventure, love, joy, happiness, and wonder. However, for many of us, we are conditioned by our surroundings, taught to comply, fit in, and often told not to rock the boat. Curiosity is suffocated in moments of compliance. Moments turn into hours, hours turn into days, days into months, and months into years. Our feelings and thoughts begin to harden with each experience. The joy of happiness found in wonderment is no more.

For years, I witnessed myself getting pulled further from my natural curiosity and passions. I was told to get a job, conform to the family life, work hard, and I was promised all of that would make me happy. Generally, I was happy because I convinced myself to believe it. Telling myself stories was the only way I could mentally survive.

As my life got a bit simpler and I became an empty-nester, my creativity slowly started to reawaken. My curiosity about life beyond my job became more intense. It is not easy to give yourself permission to explore buried sides of yourself. There is a sense of betrayal that comes to the surface. We must face that feeling head-on and fully accept it, knowing we are granting ourselves permission to come alive again. As I made peace with my past, I was able to tap into my deeper curiosity and creativity. It is part of the process of overcoming fear and doubt at the same time.

*Make peace with your past to begin to live again.*

So, how do we remain curious and adventurous as we grow older? Faith must be greater than our fear, joy must be greater than sorrow, love must be stronger than hate, and acceptance greater than denial. The power of the innate feelings we were born with must overtake our feelings of compliance.

Curiosity opens up possibilities. But, curiosity must be fueled by positive emotions, not negative ones. If each of us could hold more tightly to the positive than negative, shifts in our energy would have an enormous ripple effect in the world and cascade a positive protective coating elevating our curious mindset and feelings.

Let the ripple effect of curiosity swell into a tidal wave of energy that drowns out negativity and allows you to experience joy, love and adventure once again.

### *Be positively curious!*

What are you most curious about?

What have you been afraid to explore?

Do you feel disconnected from some of your gifts? If so, how can you rekindle that connection?

# 20.

# Intuition

Intuition is our guiding light that clues us in or warns us of something. It manifests itself in conscious thoughts, a stirring in the belly ,or many other physical ways and sensations in the body. We cannot seek it; it seeks us. We can choose to pay attention to it or ignore it.

We have been told and taught since our early childhood to pay attention to outer voices, outward signs in the world, and external physical things. Slowly, with every moment of experience, we drift away from the sensitivity and awareness of our intuition. When we ignore our intuition and settle for pleasures that temporarily satisfy our flesh, we dismiss the lessons to be learned and ultimately may have to endure pain for those temporary pleasures.

Intuition is the inner compass showing us the direction to our growth lessons in life, cleverly crafted to expedite our learning and accomplish our purpose here. However, so often, we don't recognize the messages we hear; we get confused and do not follow. With every dismissal, we encounter more detours – and wasted time – on our life's path.

How has your life path been detoured?

During my adult life, I thought I was in control. My mind was always thinking and anticipating the next move. In my avoidance of pain or not wanting to look weak, I would take the path of least resistance. I spent many years pleasing others, avoiding conflict, and doing things that brought me temporary – and what I now call "artificial" – pleasure. Most times, I felt a stirring in my belly, but purposefully ignored it. It was that inconvenient message from my spirit that was calling me to slow down, be cautious, or avoid a situation. *Too many times I chose not to listen.* As I reflect back, those moments only prolonged the learning process in whatever situation I was in. I had less positive impact on the world because of those detours brought on by my own ignorance.

Intuition is a part of each of us. Those who learn to hear the messages clearly from God – and heed them – experience  greater joy and fulfillment.  Inward feelings are strong when we are aligned and living out our purpose. Hearing clearly is the start, but the miraculous results come when we act on and obey the messages we hear and feel from God.

Inner peace is found when you listen to your intuition.

Certainly, voices, expectations, and temptations toward external pleasure will always be there. These experiences were set up to provide choice and free will for all of us. Without the outer world, we could not know the inner world. Like with any paradox, the whole "us" is made up of opposites. The balance or wholeness is found in knowing how and when to surrender to the outer and inner worlds.

When we are living our purpose, our worlds are acting in harmony with each other. So, there is no tug or pull from either world. However, when we are not in harmony, we will experience our intuition screaming at us. The outer world will scream and tempt us as well, but it is only when we are in our weakest pleasure state that we listen. Unfortunately, many have become so addicted to pleasure that their intuition has virtually become numb and silent. We need to become sensitive to our inner voice and heed its instructions, especially if we want to hear God's instructing voice.

It took a while for me to quiet the outer voices, so that I could begin to tune my listening to Him. Are you able to quiet the outer voices and hear God?

Our intuitive energy and God's voice will have a far greater impact on us fulfilling our purpose than anything else we could do. With every dawn, listen to connect with God's voice. Learn how to discern the difference between His voice, your voice, and the voices of others. Throughout the day, breathe and connect with your intuition to help you stay focused and live on purpose. At the moment of quiet slumber, give thanks to God for the blessings, the directions and love you got in the day.

Ask for guidance in the sacred moments of sleep that you will be healed, strengthened, and be nurtured for the new dawn. With the deep quiet nothingness of sleep comes the greatest space for your natural intuitive voice to be heard. Listen and reflect in slumber. God may choose to use this time to connect with us.

I practice connecting with God every morning before I get out of bed. I give thanks for a new day, so that I might course correct things from the days prior. I ask openly for His guidance just for the day because that is all He asks us to focus on. As I go off to sleep, the last thing before I turn my mind off is a quiet grateful prayer to God. It is that simple! Our awakening in the dawn will then be full of promise and passion.

**Trust your intuition, and the voice of God. For that is where your compass lies.**

How are you living on purpose each day?

What is your intuition telling you? Are you listening?

Do you have a regular practice of connecting with God and your intuition?

"Your vision will become clear only when you can look into your own heart. Who looks outside, dreams. Who looks inside, awakes."

--Carl Jung

# 21.
# Visions

Have you ever wondered where visions come from?

Yes, visions come from your imagination. But where does the imagination conjure up an idea? Visions come from deep within one's self. They were created before we were born, as seeds of thoughts, waiting to be plucked from the mind's eye.

Visions are stirrings of the soul that cannot be silenced.

Fear is stronger than one ever imagined and often wins victory over visions. Fear only gathers power from threatening beliefs in oneself. It fights and chips away at the potential superpower that exists within. Most times it wins the war and imprisons the creative soul. It is the negative voice inside your head that is constantly telling you, "No way!"

*Fear imprisons your soul!*

I have had visions for my life starting from an early age. Have you had them, too? Mine were lofty and seemed unrealistic to everyone around me. Unfortunately, I did listen to those outside voices and allowed the seed of fear and doubt to be planted in me. It took over my creative spirit and shut down my visions for a long time. Until one day in my mid 40's when I got this idea to start coaching! I was still in Corporate America, but I could not shut down the visions that would come periodically in my sleep or in my daydreams. Pure visions will not be shut down.

When the creative imagination holds true to its existence and the soul's roots are planted in purpose, it clearly rallies victory over fear. That is what I experienced with my visions. In fact, nothing but fear can stop the creative vision from becoming real. Visions *can* come true, having first been imagined in every detail.

However, visions created by the anxious mind beckon fear, doubt, and worry. This becomes real too, just like you chose to imagine. We get to choose what to fuel with our energy. We must learn to shut down those negative voices and not fuel them any longer.

Visions fueled by the positive, purposeful, and hopeful creative imagination give rise to discovery of true purpose and joy. For this is the fuel that nurtures strength of the idea. When positive imagined thoughts draw out fear, fear slowly fades and the power of purpose transforms.

I have witnessed this in a significant way in my life. As I began to crave a deeper connection with God and a greater yearning for fulfilling my purpose, my creative visions would not stop. It got to a point that somedays I was on creative overload and I began to think I was crazy.

One day I started to hear, "Yes, you can." A profound shift. Three words, driven by the imagination and the desire to live on purpose. Yes. You. Can.

When it comes to visions, everything must be imagined first before it becomes real. Immerse yourself in positivity so that negativity does not creep in and hijack your creative spirit. Feel free to talk to those negative voices in your head that attempt to shackle you. Correct them by telling them the truth: "Yes. I. Can."

### *Use your imagination for good in the world.*

What visions have you had that need to become real?

What visions have not served you? Can you reframe those visions? Or do you need to reject them altogether?

Record your visions in a journal. Evaluate them. Which ones can you start realizing today?

# 22.
# Home

A home is love and a house is just a thing. Personal property is just stuff. Memories are the real personal property that no one can steal and are more valuable than anything else. Family is not replaceable and any time is the time to make up and mend hearts. Home resides in the heart, not on a physical property.

It only takes someone passing away for us to realize that, as their spirit enters a new realm, their house (both their body and their physical house) is empty. Yet, home still remains for those who transition into heaven.

*Home resides in the heart.*

Life holds no guarantees of tomorrow. We are only promised today with family, so reach out and love your family and friends, despite their differences. Connections are the glue that centers the heart and solidifies the spirit to feeling home. Home with friends is the moment that you reconnect after many months or even years, but it feels like no time has passed.

Home is a state of mind that you treasure every day. It requires you to enter into conversations with a loving mind and a non-judgmental attitude. Home is love of others, no matter what transpires and is always encouraging, despite the circumstances.

Treasure family for you never know when you will not have one. Family history is important. People who have come before us have helped shape us and helped create our uniqueness. Ask parents and grandparents about family before it is too late. Family is woven into us regardless of the craziness that exists. People shape our lives, so we should embrace and love them, in order to learn and grow from them.

These are realizations I had after my mother passed away in 2014. It only took a day after her transition, when we were clearing out her house, to realize what home was. As my sister and brother were reunited with me after many years of disagreements, I could not help but be consumed with love and joy. The material things became meaningless to me, as I grasped for pictures to hold onto tightly. Old photographs were the trigger for my memories. Despite the past wrongs and dysfunction in our family (and whose family is entirely functional?) it melted away, as we hugged onto one another.

God tells us not to judge, lest we be judged. Everyone has emotional baggage and "issues" we call "stuff." So, we must learn to simply LOVE their uniqueness and their 'stuff'. For this is the human element in a spiritual existence. If you think you can escape it, it will chase you longer and harder until you are crippled by this reality.

*God commands us to love.*

You and I can start loving others by recognizing that God loves us (John 3:16). Everything else will follow. There is a precious peace that comes over me when I live in a space of love – of feeling loved by God and loving others with His love. Sometimes it is difficult to do, but I guarantee to love is much easier than to choose not to love. I do not want to live without that peace in my soul. Once you have experienced it, it is contagious. I often find myself telling others to seek a loving, non-judgmental heart, for it will change your life.

### *Start loving others by first realizing you are loved!*

What "stuff" in your life do you need to accept and even be thankful for?

What is it that irritates you about your family and how can you forgive and begin to accept them?

What are the elements of Home that resonate with you?

# 23.
# Life in the Fast Lane

Why do we constantly seek the rush of activity?

Okay, not everyone does, but once you are on that adrenaline rush it takes a bit to unwind. Vacations should not be the only time we stop and breathe. In fact, vacations can often be just as busy as our everyday lives.

When do we stop and learn to just do nothing? The information overload we have created for ourselves, constantly spins in our minds. As stationary as we are physically, our minds are always churning, thoughts always speeding through our heads. The fear of missing out on something keeps us going, even if it is meaningless to us. *How crazy is that?* Technology allows us to always be "on" like a light switch or a constantly blaring television set that no one is watching. Can you turn it off? I know I have a hard time tuning out.

Integrating slow time into your week is essential. Our souls need time to recover from the worldly business. Our minds, like an overheating machine, require resting moments to reassess and rejuvenate. Slow the mind, the body, and soul, through regular sleep, reflection, and meditation.

*There is beauty in doing nothing!*

Agreeably, the thought of "doing nothing" is scary for some of us. We can't imagine how to fill that "dead space." But, just lounging in a chair on the beach is a start. No reading, no listening to music, having no stimulation other than that of the wind and waves caressing your soul; that is doing nothing. If only sitting in quietness in your backyard and being one with nature were as easy! Try it!

For years, I lived my life in the fast lane. With no reason to detour to the slow lane or go off-roading, I would find myself going faster and faster. It was the day I was struck down with a seizure and cardiac arrest at 40 years old, that I realized I better find times to stop and get out of the fast lane. I began to take nature walks, quiet baths, schedule massages, and even sit down to read a good book to pull my brain from its daily momentum. Vacations became slower, despite having two teenage boys. By slowing down myself, I was able to teach them to slow down, too. Today, I cherish my downtime. I have learned so much from being present in nature and living more in the moment.

By reflecting, I'm reminded that the oceans beckon the soul to the calm and quiet of nature. The warmth of the sun, the smell of salt, and the sound of birds chirping are all reminders that we are part of something larger than ourselves! To connect with what is larger than ourselves, we have to start feeling comfortable, now and then, with doing nothing.

### *Enjoy the rush of doing nothing!*

Do you find yourself living in the fast lane? Why?

In what ways can you slow down a little every day?

What are the personal benefits of slowing down? List them here:

# 24.

# Live Happily

What does it mean to live happily?

Smile when you wake up. Laugh often, even in the midst of challenges, or for no reason at all. Hug everyone; just the request to give a hug might turn someone's pain into joy! Skip down the street, especially in the rain. Why not? You won't melt.

Find a nice comment to say to everyone who crosses your path. It is fun! People don't expect it. Breathe throughout the day and tell yourself, "You've got this!" Say "thank you" more times than seems possible. Believe it or not, it is possible to be thankful for everything.[8] Find something that makes you uncomfortable and go for it. Overcome the obstacle. It will you amaze you how easy it is to do and how happy it makes you feel. Sleep well...treasure the silence!

A few years ago, I just woke up and thought to myself, "Why can't I live happily?" Then it hit me! It was my choice whether or not I lived happily. No one person could bring me happiness or help me live happily. I needed to do it myself. As I set out to be happy, I found it easy to do when I would just focus on the day I was in. I practiced being present and appreciating the little things around me.

Smile from the inside out!

Happiness is possible every day when you treasure the smallest of experiences and feel that they are enough. With enormous gratitude for the tiniest action, pleasure, or blessing, you will find happiness in living.

Focus on sharing your happiness with others. Your mere happy presence multiplies the happiness in the world. Nothing is too small or too big to share. A simple smile, a hug, or a compliment, can have a lifelong impact on someone that you least expected.

Happiness is a very personal choice and once we decide on it, we can then share it with others. Happiness does not start from the outside and trickle in. It isn't dependent on our circumstances. It's a mindset. It starts on the inside. The gift of sharing your happiness with others acts as a spark to ignite happiness within that another person.

---

[8] The Bible instructs "Be thankful in all circumstances, for this is God's will for you who belong to Christ Jesus. (1 Thessalonians 5:18).

*Ignite your happiness inside.*

What things do you do each day that make you happy?

How can you begin to share your happiness with others?

How can you practice living happily?

# 25.
# Live Creatively

I tend to see things in color while others see black and white. How about you?
I believe I was given the craving to create something every chance I get.
God has shown His creative side to me and I believe it's so that I might follow His
example and live creatively.

When I look up at the sky and see rainbows of color or passionate fiesta
sunsets, I feel that is God showing me the way. On mornings when birds of all
random colors fly by my porch and sing a beautiful song, I am certain that is God's
creative work at hand.

*Nature is full of His creativity.*

In creating us, God has asked us to live out our creative lives! For each person
who answers His call to create, the artistry is expressed uniquely.

Living out your creative self is often hampered by doubt, comparisons, and
judgment of one's self. But stop comparing yourself to others and doubting your
ability to be as creative or as skilled as someone else. Simply realize that you are
unique. That is God's plan. He created each of us differently and we were never
meant to be carbon copies of one another. Through our weaknesses or inabilities,
He creates *through* us. That is the beauty of recognizing our limitations, yet seeking
to be creative in spite of them.

Accepting your uniqueness is what allows for the flow of creativity! I
encourage you to express yourself, through words, music, color and or through
whatever way you are called. Inspire others to live out their unique selves to the
fullest as well.

**Express the positive energy in your creative work;**
**let yourself flow!**

Are you content with the creative side of yourself?

What kind of creative spirit are you?

What are your unique gifts?

# 26.
# May I Hold Your Heart?

May I hold your heart?
With a simple glance, smile, or wink, we extend our hands and our hearts toward others. With a step forward to help another, with a comforting hug, with a laugh of delight, we express love and without spoken words, we say "May I hold your heart? May I hold your hand?"

Another soul must trust and believe that we will safely hold their heart and hand before they can really believe we love them. That is the art of connecting. The most protected part of my body – and yours – is the heart. However, our souls are what we often expose to the world without protection because we are so desperate to be loved.

Hearts survive the wounds of rejection, loss, criticism, and lies. Hearts beat on in physical form, but often stop beating in the soul. The more wounds inflicted over time, the more hardened the heart becomes.

I discovered my soul had been crushed after constant rejection, pain, and loss. I found my heart struggling to trust, even though I felt I had healed my heart. I needed comfort and healing for my soul in order to move forward in my purpose.

Hands often guide, support, share, and represent security. Hands can also destroy, attack, damage, and inflict pain. Hands are the outward manifestation of the heart that is concealed. The soul's hands are the wings of encouragement, the cradle of protection, and the tender expression of love.

That is why we must extend both our hearts and hands in sincere love toward one another. You or I cannot physically extend a hand in earnest with a broken or hardened heart. It is impossible to trust with the heart if the hand of support is not open to be held.

A great expression of love is to vibrate positive energy from the heart and extend your hand to someone and say, "May I hold your heart? May I hold your hand?"

*Extend your heart and your hand to someone.*

What is the condition of your heart? Is it hardened from being broken? Or is it soft and pliable?

Who can you choose to extend your hand and heart toward?

Is there someone you are having a difficult time getting close to? Could it be that they are having a difficult time opening their heart and trusting again? Why do you think that is?

# 27.
# Me, Myself and I

Me. Myself. I.
Well, that is one scary combination.

For most people, the thought of being alone with one's own self is terrifying. I found it scary at first, too. I struggled, realizing that my identity was bottled up in others and I no longer knew who I was.

I spent much of my life taking care of others. I would care and befriend my grandfather, then my mother, sister and brother. Soon after college, it became the man I was to marry. I was taking care of others to please everyone around me. When I became a mother, my focus shifted to caring for my sons. It was not until I was 40 years old that I realized for a fleeting moment that I had gone through life not caring for myself.

Wow! What did *that* mean?

Not realizing how desperate I was to take care of others in order to avoid taking care of myself, I jumped into relationships and addictions of all sorts. It was not until the second marriage dissolved and my kids were heading to college that I realized that God was telling me to take care of more than just my body; it was my mind, body, and soul that required attention. I had run so fast and worked so hard to please others that I had drifted far away from my spirit that was desperate to be heard and cared for.

*You must know how to care for yourself before you can truly love and care for others.*

I am a woman. I am a mom. And I am so much more. "I am Jacquie" is what I know now. I must just live openly and honestly as God guides, finally relinquishing control, power, and ego over my loved ones and over things. I realized I had to humbly extend my apology to others for trying all those years to be more than I am.

This is my prayer today:

*God, may I be open to the miracles and message that come with every day. Help me to see that it isn't up to me to care for everyone. Care for me, and help me to care for myself and to care for others as YOU lead, not as I presume. I choose to love and live for today – healing with every breath and growing stronger in my spirit with every blink. Help me to heal and be myself, without the need for others' approval.*

Life can be challenging when we are juggling the demands of others. Without a roadmap, we must improvise every day. Although it may result in disappointing others, we must prioritize caring for ourselves and for those God has entrusted in our care, before trying to help everyone else who has a need.

Journaling or spending time in quiet reflection at the start of each day might help you solidify the commitment to have a positive fulfilling day, regardless of the expectations or demands of others. This idea of caring for yourself in order to better prioritize caring for others means you are equipping yourself to be strong enough to serve. We need to find ways to be with our own self, in order to know and care for ourselves genuinely.

**You must allow for nurture of your own soul before you can nurture others.**

How do you feel when you are by yourself?

Why do you suppose you feel that way?

What new habit can you practice each day to ensure the nurturing of your own soul?

# 28.
# Mold Me

I did not always understand that I was being molded with every decision I made. The question is what do I want to be molded into?

At times my decisions and actions were molding me in a direction I ultimately didn't want to go. I detoured a lot when I was trying to be in control of my life.

Have you found that the detours in your life have happened because you were trying to control everything?

After too many detours and painful lessons, I finally decided to listen to God and let Him mold me into what He wants me to be. I do not know the map, the next step, or the plan, but He does. What I do know is that I am being molded every minute, by every quiet choice I make. Thus, I want those choices to be good ones. And so I lean upon God's direction so He can control the molding process.

It is not a forceful act of molding, but an organic process led by God. It requires surrendering to the end result regardless of whether you can see the process or know the results. This is scary for most! The more I listen, the more I am molded and transformed to my delight into the person and character that God has ordained for me since before I was born.[9]

Picture yourself as a mound of clay at birth! That clay is molded through circumstances and choices through the years until we surrender our lives to God and He then molds us into the perfect image of His Son, Jesus Christ. Each molded creature is unique in form, beautiful in expression, as God does His work in each of us.

Many mistakes along the way and reformations are required in the process to ensure that the greatest expression of beauty is formed. This is the beauty of transformation when we are willing to be molded by God into our best self.

Moment by moment decisions mold each of us.

We are all a piece of clay molded by our life experience and choices. God has a plan for each of us. Enjoy the surrender of life to Him and trust that the most

---

[9] Ephesians 2:10 says "For we are God's masterpiece. He has created us anew in Christ Jesus, so we can do the good things he planned for us long ago."

beautiful creation is being molded through the vision that existed well before your human existence.

*We are being molded by our choices, experiences, and ultimately by our surrender to God.*

Can you surrender to God so that you can be molded into what He desires for you to become?

What do you think He might have in store for you?

What decisions or actions this week are molding you into who you are becoming?

# 29.
# The Ripple Effect

When we are fully present in each moment and realize what we do or say can impact others positively, we can have a profound ripple effect on the world.

Moments make up our life – each one small in our perspective – but with the ripple effect, those moments can each have a significant impact. We get to choose whether that moment ripples out positive energy or negative energy.

As I began to understand the impact that moments can have on my life and the lives of others, I began to choose more wisely! Every moment that I accepted negative energy from another person, and let it impact my ripple, I changed the overall atmosphere in my corner of the world. In contrast, every time I absorbed or produced positive energy, the ripple cascaded in greater momentum throughout my world.

In order for our ripple effect to be positive, we must be fully present in each moment. I woke up to this idea and immediately became mindful of thinking positive thoughts, being present, and appreciating the small, but beautiful things.

A simple comment to another person that is said out of jealousy or hatred can have a profound effect on a person's life and that of other people! Even though we do not know the effect, rest assured there is a ripple effect! No stone drops in the water without a ripple! Now imagine what a simple positive comment can do.

***Create positive ripples in the world.***

How are you leaving a positive ripple effect?

How can you take more time to appreciate the moments in your life?

Looking back on some uncomfortable negative moments, what was the resulting ripple effect?

"There is no remedy for love
but to love more."

-- Henry David Thoreau

# 30.
# The Boomerang Effect

Every day brings a new joy, a new challenge, and a new pain.
I look forward to the adventure of each day. I cannot anticipate what kind of adventures will come next, but I know they will come in varying degrees. Life is made up experiences that amount to an adventure. Sometimes I wake up expecting one thing because of my past experiences, and the day delivers a twist of something new.

Now, I keep my eyes open, looking for the blessings - small and large. I look for moments of gratitude and joy. I look forward to smiling at strangers and giving unexpected hugs to a person. If I can be a blessing to someone each day, then that is a blessing to me - The Boomerang Effect.

As I reflect back on my life, I wish I had been told this principle. I would have been more mindful of my actions toward myself and others. I did not know that my negative thoughts would boomerang back to me, so I did not always practice kindness, especially toward someone who had hurt or betrayed me.

Now, being wiser and having lived through The Boomerang Effect, I am much more mindful of my thoughts. With each day, I look for the lessons, love, and joy in everything around me. If I can have learning, loving and joyful moments, then I can give them away and receive even more.

*Be careful what you think!*

What are you putting out to the world every day? It is not what you say, but how you express yourself to others that creates a positive impact or a negative one. When we know that what we put out into the world will come back to us, we can choose to act differently.

When you and I are aware of The Boomerang Effect, our actions can be gifts to ourselves every day!

*Cast out to the world love, and get love in return!*

How do you see The Boomerang Effect at work in your life?

Looking back, how was your life changed when you were angry, hostile, or negative? How was it changed by your positive, loving actions?

What will you do differently today and tomorrow that will positively impact what comes back to you?

# 31.
# Pause

What an awkward word: *Pause.*

I say awkward because as humans we are wired today to move. In fact, the universe is in a constant state of flow. The earth is constantly revolving around the sun. We are each constantly moving, growing, changing. So, how do we pause? *What* do we pause?

It starts with our breath. We must breathe constantly. But try slowing down your breathing and pausing your inhale or exhale and notice how that feels. Suspend the flow of air through your lungs for just a moment. Pause between your words. Do you notice the quietness and energy that can only be felt with a pause? Clarity and focus of the message become easier to attain from taking a pause.

It takes self-discipline to nourish yourself with a pause. Life will continue to flow, but with a pause we adjust the sail to help guide where we are heading in life. Have you tried to suspend and pause your emotions during a connection with another? It might ensure that the flame of emotion is not out of control. Nothing is ever served positively when a fire is burning wildly. I have had to learn to pause and pace my emotions.

Thoughts are constantly interjected into our consciousness. It is when we pause between our thoughts and quiet the mind that we open ourselves up to greater possibilities. We allow the pause to create more space for more creativity. With music, the beauty of a song is in the proper placement of the pause between the notes. I hope you remember this as you create the music of your life.

When speaking, it is the pause and space that we leave between each word that creates the message. In fact, sometimes with a simple shift of one letter from one word to the next, you create a pause and a new outcome. Like, nowhere to now *here.* A simple shift of space and pause after the "w" created new meaning.

I had to take a pause in my life during my late 40s. I knew I was entering a new chapter in my life, but I was not totally clear on what that would look like. It was by frequently using the pause button that I found the peace to reflect and focus on my dreams.

When we are on "auto-pilot" it feels natural to think we are on the right path. Deciding to leave corporate life was uncomfortable for me. In fact, I struggled with what direction I should be going. I truly believe today that hitting the "pause" button allowed me to do the healing work that I needed, make time for reflection, and discover new dreams.

By making simple pauses in *your* life, you can ensure you are sailing in the direction of your dreams.

**With a 'pause' all things are positively possible and purposeful!**

Can you recall some times in your life when you needed a pause but didn't take one? What was holding you back?

How do you think your life would change for the better if you took a pause more often?

What, specifically, do you need to pause for right now?

# 32.
# Peace

Peace - what does this word mean to you?

Peace is a complicated word for those who believe in only themselves. Peace is not easy when your ego injects itself into your thinking and into your behavior!

I struggled with so many aspects of my life, that peace was not attainable. It seemed to elude me at every turn. My mother was constantly praying for peace and I never understood why. On the surface, I thought she was praying for no war in the world. Since her passing, I have discovered why she was praying for peace. She was constantly looking for acceptance and love from others. She was wrestling without peace. She was praying for internal peace for herself and others.

*Peace is driven by selflessness.*

Peace is simple when you live and love on purpose. When you live in the moment and you need nothing more than that moment. It is an internal feeling when you are content. Peace is a sacred feeling when you are doing good in the world without intent for personal benefit.

Peace is a moment that cascades over yourself when you feel overwhelmed and at a loss. It is a purpose that serves to bring people together in community. Peace describes a selfless feeling internally, that all is good, despite the tension in the world.

Can there be peace on earth? Hard to understand the expectation when there is so much hatred in this world. But, peace is 'peace of mind'. Like everything in life, we get to choose! We choose a peaceful or frustrating presence. We can choose a peaceful approach or a controlling approach in life. Life is full of choices!

**Peace on earth is the inner peace we feel each day.**

How do you define the word peace?

Do you have peace in your life right now?  If not, why?

How can you foster intentional peace in your life?

# 33.
# Perspective Matters

Our perspective defines how we live.

Subconsciously, we determine our response to the world. Over time, we are conditioned to resist pain, change, and judgment. We judge ourselves by how we differ from others.

Sometimes this inflates the ego and sometimes it deflates the ego into a state of anxiety. We insulate ourselves from pain and suffering with every turn, resulting in numbness and not living authentically.

*Perspective is a choice.*

I discovered that my perspective about myself mattered the most. It determined my thoughts, actions, and emotions.

As you and I choose to change our perspective on the world, on pain, on failure, the way we see the world changes. We can choose to see possibilities, joy, growth and blessings in every moment.

### *Your perspective matters!*

How do you perceive the world?

How do you perceive yourself?

What choices can you make to shift your perspective?

"From the right point of view, every storm and every drop in it is a rainbow."

--Henry David Thoreau

# 34.
# Forgive Me

Dear Loved One,
    Forgive me for loving you so much that I smother your voice. For being controlling and wanting the best for you without you having to experience pain. For always asking questions, not because I do not trust you, but because I am curious. For checking in daily to hear your voice. For caring that sometimes you do not feel empowered. Please understand I have done all these things out of love, despite the hurt I have inflicted on you. I am one who loves you unconditionally, no matter the mistakes you make. Please grant the same grace to me.
    Love,
    The Caring Soul

I am a parent who is in transition. I have moved from being a parent with smothering control, to a parent who loves her kids too deeply to try to control them anymore.

I have chosen to relinquish control of my children to God, as if I if I ever had any control anyway. This was one of the hardest things I have ever done. I never wanted my children to suffer, have pain, or struggle in life. As I began to understand that pain and suffering was part of the growth process, it helped me release control.

I am a mom, a daughter, a friend, a sibling, a boss, a woman. I am prayerfully transforming into who God wants me to be—a person who seeks to understand others, to love unconditionally, and to live without judgment and be a light for others during their dark moments.

I encourage you to allow God to transform you into who He wants you to be. That begins by releasing control to God, so that the next phase of your journey can be fulfilled as He has willed.

*Reduce stress by releasing control to God!*

What have you been trying to control that you need to ask forgiveness for and release to God?

What controlling behaviors are holding you back from your best and less-stressed self?

In what aspects of your life are you trying to avoid pain or suffering? Are those areas of your life you need to release to God, as well?

# 35.
# Powerful Medicine

The most powerful medicines for humans cannot be bottled up. They can be prescribed but most doctors do not even think of them as powerful or medicine! We should be getting our dose daily, more than once a day. However, based on what I have witnessed in today's society, once a day is a huge improvement and will help heal each of us. Can you guess what it is?

Most of us seek a quick antidote to cure us of our ailments. However, we have been conditioned to believe that only a pill in a bottle is powerful enough to cure our symptoms or sickness. We are told to take the pill daily or multiple times a day for the rest of our lives and then we can have an okay existence.

*Seriously?*

What if the medicine being prescribed did not exist in a bottle or tube? Would you still take or seek out the daily dosage, especially if you knew it would make you feel better or cure your illness?

The most powerful medicines do not come in a bottle. They cannot be manufactured or artificially produced. The most powerful medicines I have witnessed for curing someone are:

- sunshine
- love
- smiles
- tender touch
- eye contact
- flowing water
- fresh air
- sweet smells
- flickering light

Why do I recognize these as powerful medicines? Because they have each healed me in one way or another. I have experienced and witnessed transformation and nourishment from these elements or gifts in a way that rejuvenated feelings of hope, strength, and purpose. I have found these powerful medicines can thwart negative energy like nothing else!

I wonder if, in many cases, our health is not dependent solely on a prescribed bottle of pills. We have powerful helps in nature if we would redefine what we consider medicine and our ideas of what true healing really means. Don't ignore what is at your fingertips. It is there for a reason.

*Take in the goodness of nature to nurture and heal.*

How has spending time in nature healed you emotionally or physically?

Can you recall when love, a smile, or just a tender touch healed some broken parts of you?

Which of these "powerful medicines" can you offer to help someone in their healing process?

# 36.
# The Beauty of the Pelican

On vacation, I found myself riveted every day watching the pelicans fly. I cannot explain why I was so drawn to their beauty at the time. I think they were sent to teach me a life lesson.

So much of nature and God's creatures live amongst us to offer us hope, cause us to slow down, or teach us a lesson. My life was so busy that I was not always noticing or appreciating things around me.

Until this day, when I simply sat on a lounge chair all day, doing nothing, and starring out at the sea. My thoughts began to wander. This was a very curious day for me. I could not stop my deep thoughts from consuming me. I have to say, this was the day my writing really started to flow.

So, there I sat, quietly thinking about the beauty of the Pelican and what lessons I could learn from him.

In all its strength and power, the Pelican flies seemingly effortlessly across the shore, despite the strong winds, rough tides and gray skies. The Pelican navigates the world with his senses, always accepting the present as his gift.

Never pushed off guard, he flies because that is what he was born to do. With the wind, against the wind, and in calmness of no wind, the Pelican is just content being a Pelican. He flies one foot above the sand, one mile above the ocean, or soaring for the clouds – his choice.

What can the Pelican teach us?

The Pelican showed me that we humans – as God's creation, too – are born for a purpose. Despite the differences between us, we should play to our strengths and live our truth, not trying to crawl if we were meant to soar. For the pelican never tried to be another type of bird and we should not try to be another type of person.

The Pelican also taught me that you need to walk in your truth and not get flustered with the situations around you. He never seemed anxious about the shift in the winds; he just stayed his course.

We can choose what to do with each moment – how to think, feel or act within the span of every day. It is the times when we fly against our purpose that we experience turbulence in our lives and not the smooth sailing that the pelican always seems to have.

*Live in alignment with your purpose and you will soar like the pelican!*

What lessons can *you* learn from the Pelican? Or from other elements in nature?

Are you living in alignment with your purpose? If not, why not?

What simple shifts in your behavior or thinking could bring you closer each day to your purpose?

# 37.
# Striving

How does it feel when you are striving?

Striving is a form of control – pushing against something that is not natural or blessed. It is a mindset that requires you to believe that you are in control. Striving often involves pain, grief, disappointment, fear, worry, and jealousy. All the feelings tied to striving are nurtured in the darkest of thoughts. When these feelings surface in you, this should be the indicator that you are driving from an ego point of view, not from a loving state of mind.

I spent many years striving and not thriving. I became so stressed out and exhausted, mentally and physically. I got to a point in my life when I decided I could not survive with such stress. I realized there must be something wrong with the way I had been choosing to live.

As I strived for material things, community status, and success, the tension increased exponentially inside of my body. However, when I started living within the framework of my natural gifts and talents, the striving stopped. And the result was peace.

Thriving in your uniqueness means that you recognize egotistical thoughts, but have learned to reject them and not give power to them. Power, strength, and even joy comes through love.

Think about it. When you love your enemy, you diffuse the power of negativity that the enemy strives to have over you. It is amazing to me to witness the fizzling of negative energy in the space of truth and love. This is what Jesus said we are to do each day – love our enemies and pray for those who persecute us (Matthew 5:44).

Synchronicity is evidence of thriving moments vs. striving moments. Ask yourself if you are trying really hard to make something happen. Are you finding the situation not happening easily? If this is something that you are experiencing, you are trying to control things versus going with the natural flow.

It is the time to stop, pause, reflect and then re-center yourself to your natural gifts. Ask God to take the lead. Like when driving a car and you are constantly getting lost, ask someone else to navigate! We must do that with God. Often times, He lets us lead until we get so off course we are forced into a dead end and must ask for His help!

**_Deferring to the guidance of God is the beginning of thriving, not striving!_**

What are you striving for right now? What would it take for you to relinquish control and rest in God's direction for your life?

Can you recall a time in your life when you were clearly striving, rather than thriving?

Which of your natural gifts are being utilized to their potential?

# 38.
# The Dance

Have you ever watched water dance? It is an awesome sight.
I found myself sitting out on my dock one day, just captivated by the dance. I centered my thoughts on this sight and drifted into the dance in my mind.

The power of water is like nothing else on earth. It keeps us alive. It causes growth. It makes things green. In the morning, it never sits still and dances with morning energy to the motion of the sun. In the afternoon, the water dances to the sounds of the wind, beckoning it to follow its direction. In the evening, under the guide of the moon, the water is a submissive servant, swirling to the night energy after a long day.

The dance has a lot to teach us about how we approach our own lives. Never does the water sit still, for it knows that life is lived in each moment. It dares not stop flowing because it is Nature's calling to flow effortlessly, thus needing no rest. The dance calls us to be tranquil in its stillness of rhythm, remembering to always breathe, be moving, and keep growing, however slow or fast your energy flows.

*Let your life be an endless dance and flow.*

Are you finding it hard to dance in your life? If yes, why do you think that is?

In what space in your life could you learn to dance and flow?

What morning, mid-day, and evening routine could you start in order to experience greater joy and contentment?

"Rivers are places that renew our spirit, connect us with our past, and link us directly with the flow and rhythm of the natural world."

--Leo Tolstoy

# 39.
# Get Raw, Be Real

There is no time like now to get raw and be real.

Delaying the pain, will only makes it worse and prolong the recovery. For you will recover and be stronger than before. For the before is just an illusion of strength, control, and pleasure.

I know this because I had to get raw and be real with myself. I had to face my pain, fears, doubts, and worries. So much of what I needed to deal with were negative stories from my childhood that I had carried into my adulthood. As I worked through each chapter of my stories, I came to realize I had chosen to believe that they were true. However, I now know I could choose to believe that they were simply illusions from my past that did not exist in my present. This was a moment of empowerment and healing!

I encourage you to feel into every crevice of your being – body, thoughts, and environment. It takes courage to explore places that are dark and without clarity. No matter where the path of discovery leads, trust that it will guide you to a greater awareness. Trusting in the process of getting raw and real amongst the cloaked community reveals a strength that gives way to a glorious positive life source. It is always easier to live and act like others do than to step out into your true self. There is comfort in being common. But there is freedom in being you.

It is in this rawness that the real control, strength, and pleasure is experienced.

I found the process of self-discovery – or what I like to call the "redefining process" – brought me so much joy. It is invigorating to define who I am. I took the challenge and adventure as if I was a blank canvas, creating myself into the future, not the past. My gifts that had been forgotten, resurfaced into a burning desire deep within. New gifts burst onto the scene that I had not yet unwrapped. How glorious! Each gift with a unique purpose, yet complimentary to each other. I was the painter of my life and God was providing all the tools. He already saw the masterpiece — I was becoming what He had envisioned before I was born.

We were not born to be common. We were born to stand out in our unique genius and gifts. Over time, we take on burdens, rejection, pain, and suffering that cover up our gifts, making them undetectable to ourselves and others. Feeling the desire to be seen, in our rawness, we can choose to peel off the layers of shame, pain, guilt, and hatred. It is not enough to desire it. We must do the work of honoring every feeling, experience, and moment of joy. We must get raw.

For me, the layers were deep. Just when I thought I had gotten to the root of me, I would discover a new layer. This was God's way of teaching me patience. Like pulling off the bandages to expose a wound, I had to pull off all my layers and expose myself! Like in nature, exposure of raw wounds to sunlight and air causes them to heal more quickly. By being exposed, the wound dries and no longer hurts; sometimes it's no longer visible. Only our memory recalls it. So, I encourage you to venture into the serenity of nature daily as you take off your bandages to get raw with your real self.

Looking at an open wound can remind us of a painful moment or it can make us grateful for what we survived. We get to choose what we focus on and what we feel when we look at each raw wound. Feelings are stirred with every rip, tear, and shedding of the layers. Recognize each feeling that surfaces and celebrate them – they make us whole. Treasure the positive feelings and keep them close. And be grateful for the negative memories because they can cause us to do things differently, which can propel us toward greatness. Allowing every feeling to swirl inside me was the ultimate feeling of being alive. It was the fullness of all my feelings permeating every crevice of my being that I began to tingle. Some days the swirling never slowed down to enable the clear picture of one feeling over another, but eventually it stopped. The swirl became a steady current and flow. It was in those quiet moments that I learned to feel into the rawness of each emotion.

*Honor every feeling.*
Let the negative flow through you and the positive begin to flow through your blood.

As you fill yourself up with positive feelings, and usher the negative ones goodbye, your rawness begins to not hurt as much. For me, it became a simple nakedness that is now beauty and love shining bright. It is just like when we view a beautiful vulnerable painting of a naked body, we stand in awes. The feelings of desire, love, peace, and contentment come flooding into our being.

You will feel alive in this space when you stand exposed to the world, real and healed through the process of getting raw. We need to get raw with ourselves and live in our truth before we can truly be seen and appreciated by others. What people see are only the layers of our mask that we hide behind, not the rawness of our true self. This is one of the hardest most painful processes to endure.

**The treasure lies waiting for you when you get raw and real.**

What are you feeling that is holding you back from getting raw and real?

Do you feel like you are wearing a mask? If so, small steps of peeling the mask off, can lead to real transformation. What one step can you take each day?

What does your future-self look like?

"It is never too late to be who you
might have been."

--George Elliot

# 40.
# The Foggy Space

In the foggy space it is neither dark nor light.

The air is heavy with a wetness, but it is not raining. The sun is shining, but one must trust this idea, for there is no evidence in sight. It is hard to tell the time of day, for there is no natural indicator. The foggy space allows only a few steps of visibility. The wind is calm and rivers flow.

Yesterday was bright and tomorrow has not yet come and is still out of sight. In the foggy space one can only trust in the stillness of the present, rest in the awareness that brighter days are possible, and accept the darkness as part of the journey toward tomorrow. There is a unique beauty in the foggy space that slows the mind, body, and soul. With the lack of clarity comes questions that allow for even greater awareness when the fog lifts.

There is beauty in the foggy space.

In my journey, I have encountered many foggy spaces. I have often felt stuck and frustrated. For instance, when I first got divorced years ago, I felt stuck, worried, and fearful. I did not like the space I was in and wished every day that something would change. I was so restless that I forced action and then continued to stumble. That was not very smart!

When I began to accept my circumstances, as negative and painful as they were, I realized the beauty of the foggy spaces. I have learned to treasure these times because I know that I will see more clearly when the fog lifts.

I found that the thickness of the air slows the breath to its natural flow. The calmness and quietness of the foggy spaces urge the soul to ponder. The answers lie deep inside each of us and without the foggy space, the answers go unexplored. The foggy space blows in out of nowhere and will blow away when the time is right. We must trust.

*Trust and relish the foggy spaces in your life.*

What foggy spaces have you encountered?




Did you trust or did you find yourself anxious?




What have you learned during the foggy times in your life?

# 41.
# The Gigantic Tree

What can an old tree teach us about living?

The mature tree has witnessed the coming and going of the seasons of life without asking what is next. It has lived beyond a human's life. So, why do humans think we are more powerful than the tree? For the old tree has more wisdom in having endured the heat, the cold, the wind, the rain, and the drought.

One day, I was walking in the park thinking about my life. I was certainly finding myself more connected to nature than in the past years. As I sat on an old bench, staring at an old tree, I could not help but think about how many people had sat on that bench over centuries and what they had witnessed in the park. Then it hit me! The gigantic tree had been there many centuries prior.

*How does a tree live that long and humans do not?*

Trees are far more adaptable than humans, with much more understanding of when to bend and when to just be. The tree allows for life to go on around it, without insisting to be a part of it, fully appreciating all moments and expecting nothing. It gives of its trunk as support, its branches and leaves as shade, sometimes food for people or birds, and yet never asks "what's in it for me?" It just serves.

That was it…The gigantic tree can teach us better ways to live. We need to learn to be more flexible, patient, observant, and appreciative of what is happening around us. I believe there are many more lessons we can learn from nature if we just notice all that is around us and care enough to be curious.

**Awaken to the lessons in nature.**

What are your learning moments that have come from nature?

Are you aware of nature every day? Do you stop to spend time in it each week?

What can you change in your daily practice to shift your awareness to more of nature's lessons?

# 42.
# Persistence

Persistence is an aggravating word.

It stirs irritability in some and they end up begging the persistent person to stop. To others, persistence symbolizes a sense of hope and faith. It is an action that has multiple feelings attached to it.

How does this word make you feel?

Some days, I find a thought is persistent. If it is a thought that I look to avoid facing, it brings out the feeling of anger and irritability. Other times, I have persisting thoughts about love and my dreams, which keep me in a state of bliss, tingling all over with anticipation.

Experiencing persistence in any way or from anyone is a sign that *change* is *coming*. Because change is sometimes resisted and is inevitable when it is led with persistence, negative feelings of all sorts rise to the consciousness. Those feelings that have been buried or ignored break loose.

My persistence in action is often met with reservation by others. Rather than feeling hurt or offended by others' reservation or resistance, I keep focused on positive change that I believe will come about as a result of my persistence. I also relish the opportunity to express myself differently, so with each self-expression I have a greater chance to make a change in thought or behavior.

Now, I must note, that persistence is sometimes rooted in negative intent. Yet, there is still purpose in this kind of persistence. It took me a while to learn this, but it is meant to strengthen one's resistance to negativity. Negative persistence can also cause a positive shift in our confidence and belief in ourselves when taken to task. Temptations that only have self-serving motives fall into this very category. We are to learn the power of saying no to the temptation despite the persistence.

Learn lessons from persistence.

Your full banquet of feelings is meant to be revealed and discovered. Feelings are meant to be dynamic and ever changing, but never ignored. Persistence is the action that stirs the feelings loose. Pursue the feelings when you encounter persistence. It will change your life forever! It did mine.

*The purpose of persistence is to stir action in you.*

Do you have feelings that are persistent? What are they?




Who do you know that is persistent? Does that bother you? Or do you appreciate it?




What do you need to be more persistent with?

# 43.
# The Invisible People

Have you ever taken the time to look into someone's soul?
Or do you find yourself judging the outer shell of a person with your eyes and all your other senses?

We can tend to spend our waking moments judging ourselves and others. We compartmentalize everyone into some organized system in our mind that we created as a young child and through life experiences.

The Invisible People are those who do not even make it on our radar. We don't realize that they exist. If judgment of people is not bad enough, our minds and our sense do not even recognize their existence in order to judge them. To us, they are invisible.

As I wander the streets of New York City, they are all around me – lost and invisible. In Philadelphia, they sleep in the subways or hang out on the corners. They are not the only people feeling invisible. Many of us feel invisible to others in our workplace, in our families, in our schools.

*What's the difference? Nothing!*

I have begun to engage differently with every person I meet, regardless of their status or age in life. As I started to see the level of invisibility in the world, I have been compelled to spread love and non-judgement everywhere I go. I simply take the time to ask people, "What's your story?"

Each of us exists for a purpose. We need to open our eyes to appreciate the value Invisible People offer us.

**Every soul has the right to be seen.**

Do you feel invisible? If so, to whom?

Do you avoid asking people about their story? If yes, why?




What are some small actions you can take each day to recognize those who have been invisible to you?

# 44.
# A Download

When the downloads and messages come, it is always our choice to follow or turn away.

*My Dear One,*

*I know you are scared. I know you are restless. I see the fear in your tears and feel the stir in your belly. I have prepared you for this time in your life. You are stronger than you feel and wiser than you understand.*

*I need you to trust Me and follow Me. I have a plan for you and am preparing you for his journey. I know there will be days that you want to run from Me, but I'm asking you to trust Me. Talk to Me about your fears and reservations. You must commune more deeply with Me and go without this world for a while. It might not feel right, but trust Me. I want you to understand My plans for you before you can execute the steps. You will be braver than you feel on those days of doubt.*

*Do not rely on your worldly reference because you are not of this world. I am within You and have awoken your spirit to Mine. My Spirit has been calling you for years and I have tried to stir your awakening to Me, but you were so focused on the outer world I could only watch and guide you from afar.*

*When you would wander too far from Me, I would step in and shake your outer world, so I could get your attention. It often lasted a year or two and then you allowed yourself to get swept up again chasing fictitious things. I have never let you wander out of My sight and the plans I have for you. I detoured you to something that would teach and prepare you for this day. You never understood, but eventually followed. Trust in Me, follow Me, and I will protect you for the rest of your life. You are gearing up for My purposes for you. Rest daily, reflect daily, be in My Word to hear My voice and direction. Follow Me and believe.*

*I am excited for you!*
*Love, God.*

Listen with your heart for His download.

When we tap into our Source, and desire in our heart guidance, He answers. Life is often way too busy or we are too scared to hear what He will tell us to do, so we avoid asking.

Sometimes downloads from God are unexpected. No matter how or why we get them, He asks us to trust and obey. When they are vague and not clear with steps, we are still expected to follow.[10]

Our lives can drift off course when we do not listen and obey. I certainly have had that happen in my adult life many times, in fact, too many times to count!

Since I decided to really listen and obey God, my life has been full of peaceful days, although not without struggle and pain, at times. It is in trusting Him that I find the inner peace. How about you?

### *Trust in Him to find inner peace.*

Are you listening for God's downloads or just ignoring them?

What instructions from Him have you ignored? What were the consequences in your life?

What new habit can you do every day to ensure you are listening to Him?

---

[10] Look at how God directed Abraham in Genesis 12. God basically told Abraham "Leave everything you've ever known and go to the land that I will show you" (Genesis 12:1). Not many details there. But, oh how God blessed when Abraham followed Him in faith. Today, we can get more specifics from the Bible, God's download to those who are trusting Him.)

# 45.
# The Origin of Your Tears

Where do tears come from?
Out of nowhere they flow from the deep river of your soul. When you least expect them, they can erupt from a word, a thought, or a memory that has been hidden in darkness and trapped in silence. Tears are sometimes evidence of your soul crying out to be revealed and healed. If only we could see our reflection in our tears, like we see reflections in a calm puddle.

In my healing process, I learned to embrace my tears. Sometimes I could not get the words out to express my deep feelings; but tears others could always understand. There were days when, out of my excitement and amazement, tears would start to flow. Unfortunately, as a child I was taught to not cry. It took years for me to release all of the tears that were bottled up inside since then -- yes, there were a lot of them!

Let your tears flow freely. Our tears speak to others without making a sound. We see the struggle from within, without witnessing a fight. We taste the natural salt of ourselves as our tears drip from our eyes and down to our mouths. We feel the choking around our throat and yet there are no hands bearing down. Tears can be sweet as well when your soul laughs from the inside. Tears represent the mindset of your soul. Tears manifest our reality, no matter what is said through your words.

Tears run through our soul's veins like blood runs through our human body! Tears are your soul's way of trying to get your attention!

***Pay attention to the meaning of your tears.***

What are your tears telling you?

Do you have tears bottled up since your childhood? If so, let them flow.

Is there a deep place where you hold tears that you don't want to go? Why not?

# 46.
# Pain That Cannot Be Explained

The deepest pain within each us cannot be explained.
Deeply buried in our minds and bolted away from being revealed are the most painful experiences of our childhood. Often times, we are not clear on why these memories are lost to us. The pain remains present every day, creating fear, doubts, and sometimes crippling our actions. It is a pain that cannot be explained and we often wonder whether it is real or simply imagined.

I found it only took a picture or quick comment to trigger the pain, making me frustrated that I was unable to understand its true origin. With age, the pain became harder to explain to others and more unbelievable to the world. To me, the pain was real. I unlocked my mind to unbury the moments. With every simple reflection, acceptance, whisper of forgiveness, and full reveal of the cause, I was empowered to unshackle myself and discard the unwanted weight of those moments from my mind.

As the memories and deeply-buried wounds were unfolded and released, I felt the pain that I could not explain; my body started to come alive. The protective cocoon that had surrounded my mind and body with such a hard core of blame, slowly began to break apart. The old memories faded, the pain that could not be explained was now becoming faint and my spirit began to be exposed.

The process of self-discovery can be painful, but worth it! As a butterfly is slowly released to the world to fly, the mind flies free and the spirit soars high! Without the inner journey, it is impossible to really explain the pain. Most important is the self-discovery of the spirit waiting to fly. It is born to soar, but it is weighted down over time by painful moments. Every painful moment is like a drop of mud coating the spirit and hardening it like a shell. One drop is not able to bury the spirit, but many undetectable moments of pain that build over time can do damage. Often a word is the weapon that pierces – and releases – the damaged spirit.

As the spirit flies free, it appreciates all the good, loves unconditionally, and shakes off the drops of mud that continue to be painful moments masked as water drops.

During the process of self-discovery, I released my true spirit to live freely, without being easily wounded by the words or actions of others. Now, I stand before God, caring only about how He sees me.

I encourage you to soar as you were meant to, and do not allow yourself to be grounded by painful mud drops. Detect the weight of the mud versus the lightness of the rain. It is your choice to turn the painful moments into mud or rain. For with raindrops, the spirit is nourished and the water eventually evaporates, leaving the spirit stronger than before. But mud drops harden and transform you into something unrecognizable. The choice is yours.

### *Deep pain stirs the spirit to be able to fly!*

What pain do you not want to explain?

Is the pain so deep that you cannot explain it?

What is holding you back from exploring and releasing some of your past pain?

# 47.

# The Power of Believing

With every thought, every feeling, we choose what and whom we will believe. It is your choice – believe in what God can do through you or believe the voices of others. When you believe in what God can do through you, the everyday can be transformed to the extraordinary! Each day, we can choose a grateful heart and an open mind, thus transforming an ordinary day into an extraordinary day!

Believing in the power of what God's Spirit through Christ can do within us results in the most amazing transformation. Believing we are worthy, because of our relationship with God, is the first step in fulfillment. No one is here to validate or tell you your worth, so receive it from God and believe it.

During my adult life, I struggled with believing in myself. Sure, I believed I could do a lot of things, but when it came to doing what my heart desired, my mind would dismiss it. I would hear voices in my head telling me, "No way! You are not good enough." For years, I chose to believe the negative voices. Because I believed I couldn't, I didn't.

*Our power lies in* what we truly believe about God and ourselves.

I started to really believe in what God could do through me and I realized that for so many years I had given my power away to others. How sad was that! God had allowed me to struggle through this life lesson, so that I would never again rely on the voice of others or my own power and sense of worth. God wanted to enable me with His strength and give me a confidence that comes from Him and what He knew I was capable of. I just had to believe it!

### *We each must believe before we can Be!*

What do you believe about God and yourself?

What negative things do you need to release, so that you can start being your best self?

What part of your life do you need to believe in so it can be transformed?

# 48.
# The Power of Pain

I t is amazing how God works.

Pain is given to those we think deserve it least, but God knows there is a lesson to be learned through the pain – for those experiencing it, as well as those witnessing it.

The power of pain bonds us with others, wakes us from sleeping, and teaches us all in subtle ways. As one person encounters the blow, it weakens the spirit with helplessness, into humility and selflessness. The others witnessing the blow become a bit more compassionate, loving, and grateful.

Learn to be grateful for the pain.

My life has been full of painful moments, but haven't we all had pain? I have learned to reflect back on those moments and witness the growth that came from all of those times. Pain can be the catalyst for personal and spiritual growth in all of us. As we learn from our pain we become examples to others of survival, growth, forgiveness, gratitude, love, and joy.

*Discover the power of God's teachings, through the presence of pain.*

How do you view pain?

What are the lessons you have learned from pain?

What strength have you gained from pain?

"Adopt the pace of nature:
her secret is patience."

--Ralph Waldo Emerson

# 49.
# The Wind

The wind has no color or density, no smell or texture – it can be gentle or fierce. It is not visible by sight, yet manifests its existence through other things. The wind is peaceful and comforting when paired with the sweet scent of flowers. It is a reminder of change. It moves things forward in the direction they are meant to go.

The birds know the power of the wind and are great examples of how we should flow with the wind and accept what blows our way, whether it is gentle or harsh. The birds glide along with it and are seemingly unaware when the wind blows fiercely.

I love watching nature while I'm in solitude. I am always surprised at how the simplest things can teach me profound lessons. It's amazing and awesome to see the lessons the birds teach us.[11] They accept the wind and just live.

Remember, when life is blowing fast and fierce or calm and gentle, go with the flow, like the wind and the birds.

### *Practice just being.*

What do you see or think of when you feel the wind?

Spend some time observing the behavior of birds or other creatures. What do you notice?

What can you change in your daily routine to begin to go with the flow?

---

[11] Jesus told His followers to learn from the birds when He said: "Look at the birds. They don't plant or harvest or store food in barns, for your heavenly Father feeds them. And aren't you far more valuable to him than they are? Can all your worries add a single moment to your life?" (Matthew 6:26-27).

"It is not what you look at that matters, it's what you see."

-- Henry David Thoreau

# 50.
# The Woods

I don't think there is any more "alive" place on earth, than in the woods!
Rivers flow, quietly nourishing the earth. Birds sing as if to celebrate life. The trees stand tall, observing life around them – some with broken limbs, some bent over grasping others. Other trees have passed through this life and lie on top of others to remind us of how precious it is to be alive.

Animals dodge about collecting, eating, or storing food, hiding it from the takers in the world. They seem happy and content in the woods and appreciative of the cohabitants around them.

The sun shines and glistens throughout the woods to celebrate life and the moon takes over from the sun at dusk, yet both shine out their protective energy. There is constant energy flowing throughout the woods- Alive, patient, and at peace!

I found myself gravitating toward nature as I started my self-discovery process. If I was not by the water, I was in the woods, walking and thinking. The slowness of these spaces helped to slow me down, both physically and mentally. In the calm, I found myself in deep reflection.

*Everything in this world has a purpose.*[12]

When was the last time you took a walk in the woods or sat by the water? Is it time to return to one of those places?

---

[12] To everything there is a season, A time for every purpose under heaven" (Ecclesiastes 3:1, NKJV).

How do you feel when you are in nature?

What are some lessons you have learned by observing nature?

# 51.
# This One Day

Here's a thought: There is only *one day* in our lives.
It is the day we spend living and loving. No other day is more precious than this one day. We dream of the days ahead and squander hours reflecting on past days, but this one day is the refreshing day to start new, to experience moments, to love greatly with each thought, and to embrace the present.

For this *one day* makes up our lifetime. A life full of "one days." How we spend this *one day* creates the path that fuels this *one life!* This one day is made up of a tapestry of choices – each significant no matter how big or small.

Each thought or absence of thought fosters choices and fills this one day. This one day is precious and rare. It lasts but 24 hours, and then resets itself, never to repeat quite the same. This one day is unique in its image and its impact on our lives.

*Make your one day count.*

After my last near-death experience, I woke up to this fact that we are only promised moments, not even a whole day. Every day is a true blessing and so is the responsibility we've been given in how we live this one day. I started to appreciate the small things in life a lot more. I became more present and multi-tasked much less.

Certainly, it was not an overnight transformation, but a journey of learning to appreciate the moments. I wish it had not taken such a pivotal situation in my life to teach me this. This is why I am sharing my story with you, in hopes of you learning more life lessons the easier and faster way. For if each of us realized how significant this one day is, would we savor and spend the moments differently? How colorful would this one-day look? How much love would flow if we remembered that, in a blink, this one day would be gone!

Small and undetectable choices make each second fill the colorfulness of this one day. Wake up and embrace this one day! As you choose through your one day, so your life goes.

***Choose carefully, love carefree, and live this one day!***

What is the one thing you can begin to do this one day to become more present in each moment?

How can you encourage others around you to appreciate this one day?

As you reflect back on your "one days" and the choices you made along the way, how did your choices change your life path?

# 52.
# Live Out Loud

None of us is perfect. So why do we keep trying to be?

God said "Be perfect, even as your Father in heaven is perfect" (Matthew 5:48). But He knew it was an impossible standard for us as human beings who fall short of the glory of God. So He gave us His Son who lived a perfect life and died a sacrificial death to pay the penalty for our sins. Now, we can size our lives up to His and when we live, trusting in Him for our salvation, God actually sees us as perfect.

When you understand this truth, you can live out loud.

What does it mean to live out loud? For me, it means that I will live in my purpose passionately. I will accept the curveballs along the way and relish in the lonely spaces if God directs me there. It is praising all the good and the bad in my life, by not hiding behind the cloak of attempted perfection.

It is to live the purpose and vision God has mapped out for you and me and not be frustrated with the detours. Each experience has a purpose. Live out loud with passion and energy – showing and celebrating your purpose.

***Live out loud, not behind the cloak of perfection.***

Are you living out loud? If not, why not?

Do you know someone whom you need to encourage to live out loud?

What are a few ways that you can start living out loud today?

"I am not what happened to me,
I am what I choose to become."

--Carl Jung

# 53.
# What is a Smile?

I have been consumed with trying to smile from the inside out!
Have you ever noticed while going through an airport or other public space how distant and cold people's faces are? I feel negative vibes from walking by people with a lifeless look and posture.

*Where is their smile from the inside?* We go through life in such slow motion and without emotion and yet fast-paced in our posture. We forget that we should not wait until someone smiles at us first. We should smile at ourselves and others.

While walking through the airport one morning, I started to practice feeling happy – smiling from the inside out! I was tingling. It is such an awesome feeling! A smile is an outward reflection of love – love for God, love for others, love for life. I encourage you to practice smiling and shed some love on yourself and others!

**Smile from the inside out.**

What do you notice about people when you smile at them?

How does smiling make you feel inside?

When can you practice more smiling?

"To be yourself in a world that is constantly trying to make you something else is the greatest accomplishment."

--Ralph Waldo Emerson

# 54.
# Transforming

Commit, live, be patient, but persistent.
Focus, drive yourself, make no excuses. Set a goal, have a dream and a sight in mind. Be kind to yourself through  moments of struggle, through moments of doubt, through moments of frustration.

*Facing the truth is transformational.*

Transformation of mind, body, and soul happens slowly, but it happens. When you want more for yourself and others, it happens. We come closer to the truth as we face our deepest denials, deepest sorrow, and deepest frustrations. Face the truth and realize that it is part of who you are, not good or bad, but just you.

This seemed scary to me at first, but it got easier over time. I knew I was entering into a transformational journey and did not know what to expect. The unknown is frightening, but only when you do not trust in God. In this process of self-discovery to get through to transformation, there are days of doubt, fear, loneliness, and worry. Each new day I would wake up and re-center myself for the adventure that I knew was in front of me. The biggest step I had to take in the process was facing the truth!

Conquer the fear of facing your truth. Joy will happen, gratitude will set in, and light will shine around you. What a motivator! If you are struggling with the journey of self-discovery, trust in God to show you the truth of who you are in His eyes.

### Be brave and take the first step!

Are you in a season of transformation? If so, what do you most fear in your transformational journey?

What are the truths that you do not want to face? What is the worst thing that could happen in facing your truth? What is the best thing that could happen?




How can you encourage others to not fear transformation?

# 55.
# The Dragonfly

I have been captivated by so much that I see in nature, but nothing is quite as inspirational as the dragonfly.

The dragonfly seems to effortlessly glide across the water. It hovers over a single flower without touching it, glancing into the crevices of the petals with its enormous eyes. The fluid colors and iridescent shimmer of its skin puts me in a trance. It seems to have unwavering patience and never to be in a rush. It moves deliberately, but not in haste.

As I began to wonder why this creature inspired me so, I started to explore the ancient history and meaning behind this spectacular being. In my deep knowing, I was convinced I had some type of connection to this beauty. A dragonfly symbolizes change and self-realization; with the source of change being mental and emotional maturing, discovering the deeper meaning of life. A dragonfly is born in water and is seen scurrying across it in a natural lightness, representing going beyond what's on the surface, looking into the deeper implications and aspects of life. It always demonstrates poise and grace. Its iridescence allows the dragonfly to show up differently in different aspects of life. With self-realization, it conquers those self-created illusions of self and the ego. It represents in ancient cultures the unmasking of the real self, self-discovery, and shedding inhibitions.

We do not know the length of our life, but we can choose to live a full life.

Because the dragonfly has a short adult life, it has learned to live in the moment and live life to the fullest. With its enormous eyes that can see 360 degrees, it can see beyond the limitations of this realm and into the great universe. It can detect deceit from afar and seeks out the truth. The dragonfly flies as if light as a feather, representing the lightness of feelings and thoughts. It encourages an inspiring twinkle of positive, joyful energy out of anyone it encounters.

*Inspire others through your lightness in this world.*

It can be fun to reflect on the meaning of things and creatures that exist in this world. This can be part of the self-discovery process. What animals or creatures do you find your spirit connecting with, or being drawn to? Or ask yourself which colors make you feel energized and which ones make you feel calm. In this state of curiosity, I found that I was being drawn to investigate something that I was meant to understand more deeply. Don't be afraid to go exploring. Your spirit within is whispering to you. It wants you to discover more!

Now, through what I've learned about the dragonfly, I see the journey I have been on since birth. It has brought me to this connection with the dragonfly. While nothing of my physical presence resembles it, nor my past-self, my spirit definitely does. I am that dragonfly, transformed from a much more painful heavy and burdened spirit. I crave water and its guidance. In my age and maturity, I have discovered deeper meaning in life beyond the surface of myself. I have learned to live in the moment, appreciating every drop.

Through the process of getting real and raw, I unmasked and discovered my true self. I shed my ego which lived in the illusions of my mind. I am a change agent, a beacon of light, and positivity for others. I am being called to inspire and help others through their own transformational journey. To live lightly in this world and be an instrument of service, we must have our health and wellbeing. It is your choice to live a healthy life, like it was mine.

### *Choose the path to really living.*

What creatures in nature do you find a connection with?

Why do you think that is? Go explore the meaning.

What are you curious about in life? Have you started to investigate and explore them? If not, why not? If so, what connections to your spirit did you find?

# 56.
# Enough

When is enough, enough?
Enough embodies a powerful feeling of gratitude, joy, and contentment. It is a satisfaction with the current state, knowing the joy that comes with the smallest of moments.

The big happy moments do not necessarily bring greater satisfaction, nor can we be guaranteed a big moment. We are given micro-moments with every breath and that is enough. I think it should be enough to know we are cared for, enough to know we are loved, enough to know we can love, and enough to know that life is beautiful.

I recently found myself asking, "When is enough, enough?" With every pull toward artificial foods that made me sick or the pull to have more material things, I found this question floating in my mind. I never felt like anything was enough. I chased after so much in my life, in hopes that the one thing I would get was the one thing that would be "enough." It never was. Enough always eluded me. Thus, my chase continued. I even chased status and success and could never feel that the next level attained was enough.

Contentment comes when there is enough.

The question is, "enough of what?" Enough is enough when we celebrate our ability to breathe, smiles, and sorrows. Enough is enough when you can appreciate the darkness for the light is not far behind. Enough is enough when you can just be in the moment and savor the space.

I learned what my "enough" was. After my sons went to college, I downsized and sold off most of what I had accumulated. I realized I had been holding up the big house, the possessions, and the job, in order to feel that I had enough. I had been chasing after *things* to make me feel enough, worthy, less shamed. As I began to understand my true desires and wants, it became apparent that the "things" that I had been chasing after most of my life were not the things I truly desired. In fact, it had nothing to do with "things."

What I was desiring was a simple life. A life in which I could be more present. I desired more meaningful connections with people, to give more of my time to others, and to share more of my gifts with the world. God had blessed me with gifts that I was not fully utilizing because I was so distracted by chasing after things.

I found the shedding of my things and the refocusing of my thoughts and energy toward more purposeful work to be rewarding. I finally began to feel it was enough.

### Find your enough!

Do you feel you have enough?

Do you believe you are enough? If not, why?

When is "enough, enough" in your life?

# 57.
# Now is the Time

When it is time to close your eyes and transition, will you have lived? Often, I wonder what holds people back from really living. It is hard to say for sure, but I am convinced that many people live each day with fear, doubt, worry, pain, and scarcity. They let these mindsets control their lives instead of controlling their own way of thinking. No one gives us permission to start living a more fulfilling life. We must decide on our own when we will really start living.

It took me years to truly make the decision for myself. There is never a bad time to start living, just a poor time to stop! I say it is time now. It is the time to start living before we realize we have been dead for years – simply breathing and existing. *Now* is the only space in time that truly exists, so why wait for the answer to "When?"

*The time is now!*

When it is time to close my eyes and say goodbye to this world, I believe I will have joyful memories of life that will journey with me for eternity. My possessions must be left behind and have really not mattered, but my adventurous life has fulfilled me every day!

Life is meant to be lived adventurously. And if you have memories of adventures, I'll bet you consider that you have really lived. Adventures create a tapestry of memories that not only live on in others after we are gone, but inspire others to live adventurously, as well. Our memories live on forever in those we leave behind. Even the smallest of moments and adventurous connections with others is what leaving a legacy is all about.

### Leave a legacy of a life well adventured!

What memories with others do you hope to leave behind?

What are some ways you can live more each day?

What will be your legacy?

# 58.
# Who Am I?

"Who am I?" This is the question that we all ask ourselves. From birth, we seek this answer externally. We start to compare and contrast what we see and feel to help define common ground with others. In doing so, we start to define who we are in connection to who we are most like, what we feel we have in common, and how we act.

Outside feedback starts to fuel our inside voices to tell us "we are" or "are not" what we see. Believing in the outside voices tell the inside voices the truth of who we are, or so we come to believe. "Who am I?" starts to be defined in our body, our job, our relationships, our surroundings, our feelings, our smells, our sounds, basically all senses in our life.

How often have you told someone who they are? Just put any adjective at the end of the sentence "You are _____" and you have started to help another person define and answer the question, "Who am I?"

Think about it! How often in your day do you hear "You are _____" or "They are _____" statement? Sometimes positive, but many times negative. Sometimes truthful and sometimes false. Needless to say, the statements describe possibilities of who we might be or they define a situation having nothing to do with who we really are.

I listened to far too many outside voices and accepted too many of other people's points of view about who I was and what I should do, act, and be. The longer I absorbed others' opinions, the further away I drifted from my true self. This question kicked off my quest of self-discovery. I discovered the question of "Who am I?" could only be answered and confirmed through prayer and reflection with my Maker.

I learned we will become what we believe we are.

To accept outside input as truth without really going deep within our own hearts and souls just adds to our self-deception and identity crisis. We are not living as we are, but as someone else has dictated.

Each moment that we accept careless, outside input, we get further from the truth of who we really are. Regardless of whether we intend to receive only good and supportive descriptions of ourselves, outside comments subtly chip away at our true identity.

The answer we all seek can only be discovered by taking the time to think it through and being open to what God's Word says about us. When I discovered the answer to my "Who am I?" I found much more than I was seeking.

The answer unlocked so many more emotions and questions I ever sought out. I discovered joy, happiness, peace, love, contentment, freedom, purpose, passion, and daily direction. The answer became the armor and shield I waged war with against negative comments and self-doubt. I become resilient to outside perceptions, knowing they were not the truth. I found an inner peace that could not be explained. I drew much closer to God in the process. He became my armor, my protector, my strength. He is the great "I AM" who showed me who I really am.

"I am" is really all that needs to be captured in our words. "I am" is like telling someone "just because," stating that I exist with purpose regardless of whether anyone understands. We then begin to live in our truth, with God. Look at the shift in position of the "I" and the "am". The words switch roles and paradoxically, they take on a different meaning! A more powerful meaning! "Why I am..." is the phrase that I now insert into my conversations. I have learned I must live passionately on purpose and live out "Why I am..." daily.

We are each unique and must answer the question of "Who am I? Before we can declare, "Who I am is...!"

### Ask God who you really are – and listen.

Who are you? Is it your belief or a belief that you would like to shed and redefine?

What qualities define you? Can you answer, "who I am is…"?

What qualities do you desire to foster in yourself?

# 59.
# The Drift

Every one of us drifts. Some further than others. Some longer than others. But our heart's cry is to come back home.

Sometimes we drift away from our Creator because of the temptations in this world. Sometimes we drift further and further from our inner self toward a world of voices outside ourselves. Only when our soul screams loud enough to be heard over the voices of this world do we become awakened to our true selves and begin to reintroduce ourselves to our soul and purpose.

I have experienced this. I drifted very far from my true self that it has taken a while to return. I was determined to start living and not remain limp, unable to swim against the current of life's strong temptations.

The drift can be a few years and for some people the drift takes them into the undercurrent and drowns their soul forever!

I began to recognize the feeling of the drift and the faint calling of my Creator to my soul. Eventually I listened and screamed "Save me!" I couldn't save my own soul. It is in that desperate place that God comes to our rescue.

Call out to Him and ask Him to save you from the endless drift. The ride from there will be amazing! Instead of drifting, you'll be on a wild ride that excites every part of your mind, body, and soul!

*Scream, "I'm awake! Save me!" He will listen.*

How far have you drifted from your true self?

Are you awake enough to hear your Creator calling you?

Call out to God for your rescue. And be ready for the ride.

# 60.
# Laugh or Cry

E ach day hits us with a laugh or cry situation.
  Which response will we choose? Laughs release positive vibes. Laughter is even considered medicine. Yet, crying can be therapeutic, too.

It all depends on our mindset! Crying can draw out the pain, like puss from a wound, leaving us to heal nicely. Laughter can instill hopefulness in others who hear it.

These days I cry out of joy and out of sorrow. I laugh out of amazement and out of sadness. It is all mixed up. Yet I tend to believe that is the way it should be. As I began to explore many sides of myself, I would find moments full of feelings. I have learned that none are bad or good, they just are.

Emotions are the fuel of life!

It has taken a while for me to accept this, but when I began to live in the fullness of emotional expression, my stress was reduced, my happiness increased, and love flowed naturally to myself and others.

Emotions, whether it's laughter or tears, rev us up and slow u down. They protect us and delight us. Emotions are the best of life that is worth celebrating! Emotions help us connect with others, especially when we laugh or cry together. There is something special about the bonding process of sharing laughter or tears.

### *Celebrate the beauty of emotions!*

What emotions are you afraid to feel or share?

What emotions do you think are most misunderstood?

Who do you need to share your emotions with? Will this release some stress you have been carrying? Bring you happiness? What else?

# 61.
# One Step

It only takes one small step to set you on your way to fulfilling your life purpose. You might be thinking, "I don't know my purpose!" It does not matter. God knows! He directs you with one step at a time.

It helps me to share what I am thinking with God:

"God, I know I am listening and trying to be patient. Every morning I wake up and talk with You. Throughout the day, You whisper words to me, You send people in and out of my life to teach me something, and You equip me with one step. I thank You."

I have found myself talking with Him regularly in my self-discovery process.

One step, one moment, one thought, one action.

One step, taken blindly, will stretch your trust, faith, hope, and obedience. You may even find that love and strength help spur you toward the next step. But one step taken in fear, doubt, anxiety, and judgment, serves only to delay and detour your journey toward purpose.

God asks us to surrender, listen, and obey – SLO. These are the first three steps toward purpose. I often raced toward something with the belief that I was running toward my purpose. I quickly discovered it was an illusion and temptation formulated to distract me. With my natural adrenaline rush, I did not pause to hear God. As paradoxes have it, I was going fast to go slow! Not at all what I was striving for.

If only I believed enough, trusted without conditions, and paused more intently, I would have realized that if I went S.L.O. I would go fast! One step, in balance, harmony, and in alignment with God, requires patience. Picture yourself crossing a flowing river, slowly stepping onto one rock at a time. By focusing only on the next rock, you progress toward the other side of the river. If we watched the other river bank, we would miss the next step and slip and fall. Still recoverable, but simply delayed progress.

***One step at a time is all that God asks of us!***

Are you going S.L.O. (surrendering, listening and obeying) in order to go fast?

What daily habits in your life could you change to draw you closer to God?

What might be *your* first step in moving closer to your purpose?

# 62.
# Transitions

How do you view transitions? Difficult? Time-consuming? Complex? Transitions can hold hope, opportunity, purpose, passion, and fulfillment if we choose to look at this "in between" space as full of possibilities and not of pain.

Transitions require leaving a comfortable space. Sometimes we are jolted involuntarily into transition and it becomes easy to sink into a negative, dark, and fearful place. Other times, we have made a choice to walk toward something new and this choice provides no less fear and doubt. The space of transition is uncomfortable, even if you have a positive perspective.

Transitions are purpose-filled. It is in this "nowhere" space that a rebirth takes place – in mind, body, and spirit. When we rush to the other side of a transition prematurely, we do not grow to our potential. Too many times, in the uncomfortable state we cannot endure the pain, the unknowing, or the fear that accompany transitions. That causes us to create a false reality in our transition – false messages created from fear-based thinking, and false actions from the fictitious reality to the other side of a transition.

I have not always been patient. *Imagine that!* I spent much of my adult life trying to be in control, even during times of transition. Frankly, I was not wise enough to understand that God was in control and guiding me toward something for His purpose.

Do you try to control everything in your life? Have you looked at a seed that sprouted too early and never grew to its potential? We are those seeds in the world. We are planted in a spot with purpose. It is in this purposeful planting that we are asked to be patient, to be okay with the darkness, the unknowing, and the coldness. God plants us where He wants us to grow!

Seeds do not plant themselves. It is in being buried alive that we die and transition into someone of purpose. Throughout our lives, we are reborn multiple times, through transitions, in order to grow and be able to fulfill His purposes for us.

Think of transitions in your life as the waiting room for God's next assignment for you. In this space, we are anxious. We see others getting their assignments quicker. It is in this space that we are not yet ready to fulfill our purpose. In this waiting time, we must be open to learning daily and being grateful for the transition time. It is a time to be quiet and still. For if we do not sit and listen, we will miss God's direction and our bodies and minds will not rest enough to gain the renewed strength needed for the next phase of the journey.

*Rest, wait and learn, listening for instructions from Him.*

I have learned not to wish away the gift of transition. Instead, I choose to enjoy every day the restlessness of my heart, the pain in my body, and the quietness of my actions. I have released my desire for control and find excitement in the unknowing.

Transition periods can come in moments, hours, days, months and years. There is no set timing for release from a transition, so do not focus on the release, but enjoy and grow from the lessons received in the process.

**Transitions are purpose-filled. Don't rush them.**

Are you in a place of transition in your life? If so, how are you feeling?

Do you find yourself uncomfortable with the in-between space? Why?

What can you do daily to practice patience and trust during this process of growth?

# 63.
# One Decision, Many Lessons

Early one morning I encountered a homeless man walking over a bridge in front of me.

From a distance, he looked dirty. He seemed confused and a bit hungry. He was constantly looking at the ground for what I thought was food or cigarettes. I was convinced he was a drug addict and despondent.

As I began to approach him, my spirit became uneasy. The voices in my head were fighting. The compassionate voice was whispering *Talk to him*, yet the skeptical fearful voice was saying *Not your problem. Just walk by quickly.* Which one was I to listen to?

Every moment, we are faced with decisions.

We have two voices that constantly vie for our attention and allegiance. One is the voice of our flesh, the other the voice of the Spirit. Sometimes, the Spirit's voice – the compassionate one – is so soft that the message from our flesh – the louder, controlling one –is more clearly heard. Unfortunately, too often, we have silenced the compassionate loving voice, which makes our resulting choices self-centered. It is better to have two voices arguing with each other than for the fleshly voice to win. Never will the fleshly self-centered voice be silenced, just suppressed to a whisper.

I listened to the Spirit's voice and said "Good morning" to the homeless man, while offering a smile. He responded with a smile and said, "Beautiful morning." One thing led to another and before I knew it, I was walking alongside him, over the bridge, conversing with him.

I asked, "What's your story?" He smiled and proceeded to light up with energy, telling me about his life. His story was not what I expected. That moment I realized that a person's story is usually not what we think it is. As I was about to walk on beyond him, I asked him, "Want a morning coffee?" He responded quickly with "Yes, thank you."

We entered a small coffee house together, as friends ordering two coffees and a muffin for him. No matter the soiled clothes, the messy dirty hair or hunched over demeanor, he was welcomed. I finally got around to asking his name. (Another lesson, ask a person his or her name!) A person's name is precious to him and defines his existence.

As our coffees were being prepared, Luis told me more of his story and I learned some powerful lessons that morning. We parted ways, each offering a smile and a blessing to the other.

With one decision, I learned many lessons. I learned to listen to the Spirit's voice urging me to be compassionate, instead of assuming I know another person's story. I also learned to ask someone their story before deciding that I knew what it was.

I also learned that if we extend a loving smile to another person, we build a connection. By sharing our time, we learn. If we choose to care and hear a story, we grow in love and give love at the same time. We are ultimately connected with love.

The homeless are an invisible and abused group of people. They ask for little, yet often get a mound of abusive comments and hateful stares. I have learned through experience that many are loving, caring, and joyful people trying to make the most of their one or many poor decisions that landed them on the streets.

***We are all one poor decision away from a different life.***

How do homeless people make you feel? Why?

What story do you tell yourself about someone? Have you validated that with them?

Do you wish someone who has judged you would have asked you your story first? Think about approaching them tomorrow and sharing a coffee and your story with them.

# 64.
# Choices

We are all connected by two things – time and choice.

We each get 24 hours in a day and within that time we have the freedom of choice. Ultimately, choice is the differentiator of lives!

One of the most important choices we make is what attitude we will have when circumstances befall us. Life consists of negatives and positives. Whether a situation is one or the other is often determined by our attitude.

When we choose an attitude of faith, love, trust, compassion or honesty, it fuels positive results. Choosing fear, hatred, dishonesty, or judgment drives a momentum toward negative results. We ultimately get what we give. Positive begets positive, negative begets negative.

When we make choices with the motivation of benefitting others, and not merely ourselves, we can receive positive energy into our lives. Serving God and His desires – rather than our own – is one way to conquer the negative energy that is looking to divide and conquer us.

For much of my life, I let my ego take over. I made choices based on how they would benefit me. I chased after material things and meaningless stuff. Trying to avoid pain as much as I could, I quickly fell into a scarcity mindset, feeling like I was never good enough or that I never had enough. Choosing to understand and stay connected to God, rather than my own ego, is where positive energy began to flow.

Ego-driven decisions made out of a scarcity and fear mindset turn a person against serving, and everything pertaining to love.

The battle against negativity in this world, lies *within* each of us, not outside of us! I started to seek peace, and a positively purpose-filled life. I had to choose my attitude in each moment which determined what I spent my time thinking about. Only after a conscious decision not to feed my ego, did I start living in a way that leaves legacy imprints on the world. And that decision isn't only made once. We must make that decision every day, for ego will continually try to rise up and take over.

Time and choice are the common gifts we were given by God. Surrendering, listening and obeying God without ego is our choice. When it comes to God, you don't get to pick one or two of those actions only. It takes all three purpose-filled actions to get positive results. Without the three together, we are exercising ego's choice.

**_Choose how you will go forward with your life!_**

What choices can you make today that will be positive for you and for others?

What have you chosen to do, during your lifetime, that has served others more than yourself?

What attitude will you choose today, in spite of your circumstances?

# 65.
# Only You

Only you can know what is really going on inside your head. And only you can feel from the inside.

Nothing from outside of ourselves can ever completely heal us. Even love is expressed and felt first from within. We can tell ourselves the stories that we want to hear. We can praise and punish ourselves much greater than anyone could ever do to us.

Only we can know the secrets, pain, exhilaration, and aliveness that lurks deep within. Until we can fully share our feelings with another, without fear of being judged, we will never experience what it means to be fully alive.

Only we can say no to the inner and outer voices that pull us away from our Creator and our true purpose. Our ego will tempt us to follow it. But our ego separates us from pure love. Pure Love is what God longs for us to choose and experience. But our ego, -- our darker self – often deceives us into believing we can attain it and experience it without Him.

Love lies waiting to be embraced and followed. With our daily distractions in darkness slumber, we can become numb and dead to the feelings that create our connection to pure love.

Seek to stimulate your range of emotions. As I said before, emotions and feelings are neither good nor bad, they just are.

Feelings are meant to flow through us in every moment, not get stuck or denied their existence. As the river flows, the wind blows, and the sun shines its beams of light, feelings exist to be expressed and give life to us. simply exist to give life to us! We cannot live without air or water, just like we cannot live fulfilled without feeling.

After years of deep pain, I finally faced the rawness of what only I knew was lurking in my inner thoughts. It took a lot of trust and a desire to heal myself, to be able to endure the painful process. No one could tell me to go through the process, I needed to be ready for it. I had to crave life over death. I had to choose to find who I really was.

Only you will know when the time is right to unapologetically accept yourself.! At that very moment, you will experience feelings out of nowhere that have been buried deep. Celebrate the feelings and say yes to the wild adventure ahead of you!

God never promised that life would be easy, only that it would be fulfilling, purposeful and worth it, when we invite Him into it.[13]

### *Enjoy the ride of your life!*

What do you need to face head-on in your life?

What are the painful moments that you must choose to forgive in order to heal yourself?

What other voices do you need to shut down? Either from the inside or the outside?

---

[13] "The thief's purpose is to steal and kill and destroy. My purpose is to give them a rich and satisfying life" (John 10:10).

# 66.
# The Great Illusion

If only we realized that our perception of ourselves is just an illusion we create in our mind. It is only when we recognize the illusion that we can connect with our true self.

It's difficult for us to accept our reality and discover our true selves. For we must battle what seems inevitable to create what is possible! In the depth of our thoughts is what we tell ourselves are truths, which are simply illusions to distract us from our potential.

From the time I was a young child, my perception of myself was based on false beliefs. I carried them into my adult life, never questioning and often ignoring their impact on my life. What would my life have been like if I had just realized I could have chosen to change those beliefs?

Have you been carrying around false beliefs that you struggle to shed? We must be jolted from our false beliefs and find the Truth in order to really start living.[14]

Illusions are comforting because we can live in our own made-up reality. Unfortunately, when illusions are erected to restrict our purpose and fulfillment, we live in turmoil and pain. Pain exists to awaken us to the lies we have been telling ourselves and the fake reality we have been living in.

I have awakened to a new reality of possibilities and unlimited potential that is so satisfying, it ignites a great passion inside of me for greater truths.

Unleashing the search for truth in oneself causes a ripple effect of awakening. The more we are all awakened to our true selves, the greater the significance we will have together, and the greater impact we can make on this world!

---

[14] "Jesus told him, 'I am the way, the truth, and the life. No one can come to the Father except through me'" (John 14:6).

*Awaken from your false realities to discover the truth.*

Upon awakening to your truth, what ripple effects can you create?

What illusions have you held on to that you should shed?

What is holding you back from exploring and facing the illusions in your life?

# 67.

# The Battles

Though we are weak, through God we are stronger than we know.
     We can choose to see ourselves in our minds as weak, and therefore useless
to serve Him. Or we can trust what He can do through us and see ourselves strong
through Him because He never leaves our side. It is only when we connect to this
human space and time that we fail to see our calling. We choose to believe it is
something that is outside of our abilities and therefore not possible.

We can choose.

Everything is possible through faith in God.[15] What He wills, cannot be fought.
The battles of wills are waged between His will and our human will. It takes much
less strength to surrender and not battle against Him. Save your energies for the
fight alongside Him. Or better yet, let Him fight your battles. For our human
nature was created to battle everything. Battling against His will only serves to
extend the length of suffering and pain.

Think about our human flesh. It battles off illness. It battles daily, moment to
moment, to keep the heart beating and the lungs breathing. The brain, in its flesh,
will fight the spirit right to the end, in order not to die in this world. It is natural.

We were born to battle.

Conquering the battle within me was perhaps the most painful war that needed
to be waged. It was easier to battle outside of myself, but those were meaningless
victories. The lies I told myself, the stories I believed to be true, and the shame I
accepted, were the very things I had to silence and conquer.

Battles can only be won with love. Love for God and trust in Him. We can
think we won a battle in this world, but it does not mean we won the war. Every
time we love through the battle, to the end, the fire of negativity is extinguished.
Without love, the flames of non-truths still burn silently until another moment
ignites them again.

The most significant war had to be won against myself. It took battling daily to
suffocate the voices that I heard inside. When I realized that He was battling

---

15 "Jesus looked at them intently and said, 'Humanly speaking, it is impossible. But
with God everything is possible'" (Matthew 19:26).

alongside me, then I trusted Him to lead the way each day. I had to surrender control to Him, yet battle with Him to overcome the human voices and negative energy burning within me.

The battles are real. They are there for a purpose. When you wake up and realize that they are easily won through following and obeying God, the choice to surrender our human power to Him is easy. Winning battles that are deep within, serve to strengthen us and propel us toward the meaningful work He has commissioned for our life.

*Unconditionally love through each battle and
the victory will be swift and joyous!*

What are the battles you are fighting?


Have you surrendered and released control to God?


What do you think the lesson is in each one?

# 68.
# Best Love Ever

"Love" is waking up and being so grateful to be alive that you lie in bed with a sense of awe and stillness.

"Trusting love" is the kind of deep, devoted love for God in which you know He will alert you to something that isn't right.

"Unconditional love" is selfless love for others, regardless of what they have done or not done for you. It is non-judgment and complete acceptance of all of God's creation.

"Adoring love" is what we express to – and experience from – close friends and family. It grounds us and protects us on otherwise anxious days.

The "Best Love Ever" is the unconditional, ever-gracious love from God that propels you forward with faith and repels all fear. For knowing you are loved like this makes nothing impossible.

**_All things become possible when you know the Best Love Ever!_**

What kinds of love are you familiar with?

Which of these kinds of love would you like to express and experience?

What would it take for you to begin experiencing the Best Love Ever?

"To love at all is to be vulnerable."

-- C.S. Lewis

# 69.
# Vulnerability

The newborn, fresh from the womb, is completely vulnerable. Totally weak, not able to defend itself, unable to speak, and totally naked to the world, the newborn lies helpless for days, collecting unconditional love and affection by doing nothing but being vulnerable. The tiny newborn trusts and believes it will be taken care of and knows no worry, fear, or desire to control.

The pure sense of one's being is discovered in the space of vulnerability. What a beautiful condition this portrays to the world. There are moments in our lives as we grow older that we are vulnerable, but have learned to look at it as a negative state of being. We have been conditioned over the years to clothe ourselves, hide our true self, trust no one, fear change, and strive for control.

For if we were naked and our true self relinquishing power to someone, what would that look like? For many, this describes the art of making love with a husband or wife. Amazing! The gift that God gave us to make love to one we have committed ourselves to in covenant marriage, brings us back as close as one might come to our purest state of vulnerability.

When a natural disaster hits and a person has lost everything, they suddenly feel raw and exposed to the community in which they live. They must rely on the unconditional love of others to rebuild. That is vulnerability – and another way God asks us to be okay with vulnerability.

When sickness hits a person out of nowhere, despite our desire to want to control, the illness forces the nakedness (helplessness) of one to others and the reliance on their support. It usually brings a person to a state of deep reflection in which they expose their raw emotions. This, too, is a beautiful example of vulnerability.

Throughout our lives, God allows moments for us to experience vulnerability. In the purest form, He seeks to bring us back to Him through our vulnerability. As He birthed us out into the world in pure vulnerability, it is our life journey to learn and accept how to be purely vulnerable once again. Vulnerability attracts the state of unconditional love and non-judgment in its purest sense.

I wonder sometimes if God chooses to be vulnerable everyday with each of us.

Despite us rejecting Him, judging His intentions, blaming Him, declaring hatred toward Him, and so many more negative actions, He remains gracious toward us. In some ways, I see that as Him choosing to be vulnerable with us. Always exposing His unconditional love, His truest being, and at times seemingly relinquishing His control as He gives us choice and free will. All the while, we fight for our will. For us to be truly vulnerable we must ultimately love God, love others unconditionally, and relinquish our control to God.

Living in this state of vulnerability takes trust, faith, patience, love, and acceptance. It is no different than how nature exists. God has provided examples throughout our world for us to turn to and model that state of being. A sapling is completely vulnerable at its start of growth and despite remaining vulnerable, often grows into a beautiful tree that lives for centuries. Wow! Pure vulnerability! The sapling turns over its life expectancy to God and gratefully accepts each day it is given.

Vulnerability is paradoxical to how we have been taught to live. Yet so many truths rest on the opposite of what we expect. Ease into a state of vulnerability and live a fearless, loving, happy life!

### *Vulnerability is power, not weakness.*

Are you comfortable with being vulnerable?

Do you see a connection to vulnerability and how you feel about yourself?

How can you start being more vulnerable with those whom you love and trust?

# 70.
# As the Birds Live

Seek to live as the birds live.

It is apparent that they live in harmony with all other nature. They recognize each other's distinctive beauty in the differences of their color and sound.

Birds go with the flow of the day, waking up early with the dawn to sing their songs of gratitude. They fly around to move their bodies and awake all their senses! It is as if they are doing yoga in the sky. They flow through the air, sometimes dipping, other times gliding, but always breathing!

Birds go about their day not worrying about tomorrow, but only the moment they are in. They exist without judgment of others, and sing songs of love. They collect food for only the day's ration and prepare shelter for the night. They commune with one another, resting on a wire or a branch and exchanging stories of the day.

Giving no power to the strong wind blowing or the falling rain, birds still flow throughout their day. They understand that there are sunny days, cold days, foggy days, and dark days. Their spirits know that it is but a moment or season and will pass through to the next natural beautiful gifted environment. They recognize the beauty in every moment!

Birds have a curious nature that keeps them flying about, exploring and chatting all day. They know that the energy flows throughout nature and they are of nature, so they must flow. They pause only for a moment now and then to soak in their surroundings, perhaps appreciatively.

As the birds live, so should we live. Be mindful each day of the birds around you. They are placed in our presence for a purpose – to remind us to breathe, live, and love in nature's way.

***Observe and live as the birds!***

What do you find most interesting about birds?

In what way would you like to live like them?

.

What is one small change you can make today so your life resembles the simplicity of the birds?

# 71.

# In the Rain

It is in the rain that we are soothed, cleansed, quieted, and rejuvenated.

The grayness of the sky invites slumber, and a sense of slowness. Calm and silence is felt as the drops scatter over the body and over the earth. Enjoy hearing the chirps of the birds as they awaken to the dawn, cleansed and tickled with every drop. Oh, the joy and positive energy that waterfalls the earth when the rain pours down.

Rain is nourishment for nature and for our souls, if we take the time to slow our energy to the rhythm of the drops. It is in this rainy period of life that we are being prepared for refreshment and re-emerging sunlight that will bring us a new vibrant energy.

Our energy is not always sustainable for long lengthy days. We must appreciate the rainy days in our lives as a pathway to rejuvenation and a greater purpose and impact. In the rain we learn to appreciate silence and the pause of life.

Nature is our example of how to celebrate and live in the rain! Flowers jiggle, leaves turn to the sky to absorb as much wetness as possible, the grass gets mushy and giggly as it shines bright green. Nature comes alive in the rain!

### *Embrace what the rain can do for you!*

How does rain make you feel? Why?

What does the rain inspire you to do?

What do you notice throughout nature when it rains?

"Isn't it funny how day by day
nothing changes but when you look back
everything is different."

-- C.S. Lewis

# 72.
# Connections in the Moment

Some people come into our lives to be blessings. Some just for the moment. Others for longer.

Even the momentary connections, like passing by a homeless person, can teach us humility, gratitude, and compassion.

When some people come into our lives in a moment, we realize they have the potential to be someone we continue to connect with – for a day, a week, month, year, or more.

Every day we can realize the value of connections in each moment. If we are truly present in the moments that we connect with others, we can deepen or lengthen those connections. Feeling and utilizing all our senses ensures the greatest success of connections in each moment.

Even to be still in the moment with yourself, allows you to connect with yourself and your intuition. Being silent in your being, including your thoughts, creates an inward temple that is able to host a relationship and conversation with God. We assume that prayer is actively talking to God, but true prayer is a relationship in which there is a two-way conversation – talking and listening to God as He talks.

We must create silence to allow God to speak to us and for us to listen. This silence can come in moments of reflection, meditation, and quiet waking moments before rising out of bed. It can also come as you rest into your pillow at night. Some find that nature walks in silence make them feel more connected them to God. Other physical activity done alone can be equally conducive to God connections.

Connections in each moment can impact our life path. Our attitude is part of the life path combination. Connections in each moment can be viewed as negative or positive, never really neutral. Failures and other painful moments can be viewed positively as lessons, or negatively as punishment.

Sometimes positive moments can eventually turn into painful moments, like a loving relationship that eventually goes bad. We can learn from both positive and negative experiences. Having a positive growth and learning mindset, listening, and being present will be the ultimate energy combination that will maximize the connections in each moment!

*Don't waste an opportunity to connect in the moment.*

Is there a momentary connection you've been avoiding? If so, why?

What are some momentary connections that turned out to be significantly impactful on your life?

When have you been a positive momentary connection for someone else?

# 73.
# Love Enough

I am enough. I am enough because I was lovingly created and intricately
designed.[16]

I have come to understand that no matter who tells me I am fat, ugly, lazy, or
any number of other words used to attack me, I am enough and I am
unconditionally loved by You, God. You only want the best for me. You fill me
with a sense of purpose and You allow me to learn what I must in order to become
more like the Image of Your Son.[17]

I understand that You bring people into my life to teach me lessons. I must
keep my eyes open, my heart exposed, my ears alert, and my mind non-judgmental.
With each new moment or experience, I grow closer toward or further away from
You.

I detour and derail my progress, or move steadily toward fulfilling my calling.
You have provided gifts for each of us so that we can use them for You and thus
fulfill our purpose. I accept willingly and gratefully the gifts You have given me,
even if they aren't the same gifts You have given to others.

Help me to remember – on the days that self-doubt, negativity, and fear set in –
that I am enough. I am enough because You are enough. And because I am loved
enough.

---

[16] Psalm 139:13-4 says: "You made all the delicate, inner parts of my body and knit me together in my
mother's womb. Thank you for making me so wonderfully complex! Your workmanship is marvelous—
how well I know it."

[17] Romans 8:28-29 says: "And we know that God causes everything to work together for the good of
those who love God and are called according to his purpose for them. For God knew his people in
advance, and he chose them to become like his Son...."

*His love makes us enough!*

What are some of the labels people have put on you?




Can you begin to live according to God's labels for you?




Who can you encourage today with the message that they are enough because they are loved?

# 74.
# Direction

What direction is your life taking?

Direction indicates the way one is headed. But your direction today does not necessarily determine your final destiny.

That's because we can choose to change our direction at any time.

Sometimes we are headed in a certain direction, convinced that is the right way to go. But what seems like the right direction for some, might be the wrong direction for you and me. But all is not lost. Realizing one is going the wrong direction can give clarity to one's final destination.

Directions are moments in time and not lifelong maps. If we don't go the wrong direction at one time or another, we are not equipped to share with others our experience or empathize with another who has chosen the wrong path.

We can learn from wrong directions and then course-correct.

As long as the destination is our focus, then direction is simply temporary. From one moment to the next. Focus on the destination and be prepared to modify the route along the way. Live off the grid for a moment, direct thoughts to the past, but keep flowing in the direction of your destination!

### *Keep your eyes on your destination.*

When have you known, without a doubt, that you were going in the wrong direction?

What were you able to learn from that detour?

What detours can you take right now to get you on a closer course to your destination?

"Not until we are lost do we begin to understand ourselves."

--Henry David Thoreau

# 75.
# Being Touched

There is power in being touched.

When one hand meets another a connection is made. There are so many ways that we are being touched throughout our lifetime. You know it when you feel it! The most obvious touch is a physical touch between two people. Not always as impactful, but a connection nonetheless. Hugs, kisses, handshakes, and holding are all ways that we are being touched.

The more powerful – and sometimes less obvious – ways we are touched is through the energy that we exude out onto others. The subtle glance of one person's eyes creates a touch, either warm or cold. You can feel that connection without anything physically happening.

Have you ever walked by a person on the street and felt a connection that you cannot explain? You have been touched! Being touched by a person's kind words draws out a warmth inside me and a smile on the outside. Feeling the warm breath from a lover on my skin, I am touched with desire beyond the skin. There are so many forms of being touched that light me up from the inside, like feeling raindrops on my skin or the ocean waves caress my body. As I discovered the power of touch, it made me want to practice touching lives every day.

The power of being touched is transformative. A touch shifts feelings, desires, physical form, and mindset. Watch for the signs when you touch another person. Before we were born, we craved the connection to the water, sounds, warmth, and nutrients to give strength to our spirit. At birth, being touched for the first time physically bonds a mother and baby. The delicate baby's lips sucking on the mother's breasts, gives way to an amazing sensation for both. Being touched is a universal and natural need. When we deprive ourselves of moments to be touched by another, our inner and outer shell begins to harden.

For many years, I was reserved and did not open up to others – I did not allow myself to be touched. Over time, I became so hardened that it took a lot of touching to melt and soften my spirit within. The power of being touched is so transformative, that often with a smile or a loving kiss, the heart becomes soft again.

Being touched by the cooling wind, the warm rays of the sun, the sweetness of soft flower petals, melts away the hardened elements of the day. The feel of grass on our feet or the moonlit sky on your backs, connects us to something beyond ourselves. That is the power of being touched!

God desires to touch us in ways that we cannot even imagine. Next time you allow yourself to be touched by someone, know that it is God working in your life. He connects us to others, to nature, to life beyond our own self. Connections that magnetize us and draw us to experiences and feelings perhaps we never knew existed within – those are connections to Him. As His touch began to melt away the hardness of my spirit, I could begin to really feel Him in my life.

There is no greater positive impact you can have on the world than touching others with your love, creativity, your words, physical presence, caring demeanor, and positive energy. Being touched by others in the same way creates a powerful connection beyond the physicality of life. Our imaginations soar to "all is possible beyond the impossible." Ultimately, touch manifests love in its rawest and real form. Be love, give love and get love. Connections are powered through being touched!

### *Feel God's touch on your life.*

Do you enjoy being touched or does it bother you? Why do you think that is?

In what ways have you been touched, significantly, by someone?

In what ways have you been touched by God?

# 76.
# Silence

What is silence?
It is so far removed from our everyday chatter that we can hardly relate to the space. Yet, silence is the only space to think, to appreciate, to experience gratitude, and to honor love.

Silence is a distant cousin to the busy self we become. With each day, we honor noise and business over silence. Silence is the stepchild of forgotten time and space; when we have "extra time" we honor silence.

Silence is the medicine that we refuse to take because we don't know its side effects. But if we trusted enough, we would gobble up silence as a "snack food" or treat that we cannot get enough of.

Silence of mind, space, and presence is a sweet gift from God that we tend to believe is poison and refuse to swallow. But silence is not threatening. It is not something that we need to fill with noise or empty talk. Silence paves the way for us to hear the voice of God.

It took me a while to appreciate the gift of silence. My life was so busy that there was never silence. I was talking a lot or I was listening to others. Frankly, it was scary at first to be okay just sitting with the silence of your own thoughts. Thoughts are not always good ones, so I found myself anxious about what ideas would pop in to my head. After a daily practice of silencing my brain, I realized that silence was the very place that I could find healing, tranquility, and peace. I treasure it now.

***Don't shy away from silence. It can speak wonders!***

How comfortable are you in a silent room?

What is your natural instinct when you encounter silence? To enjoy it or avoid it?

In what area of your life could you use more silence?

# 77.
# Alive Beyond Existing

As my breath flows, I wonder what it means to be alive. I smile and feel my heartbeat. Am I alive? I think I am.

Many days I spend socializing with my family and friends, which brings me a sense of aliveness, until turmoil or tension set in. Then I either retreat into quietness or absorb the rage around me.

The gossip and judging comments about others, the weather, the world, just keep me swirling in a sea of confusion. Frustration, anger, resentment, and hatred are all energy fields that look to captivate me into believing this is real life. Negativity is such a familiar feeling that it actually connects negative people with other negative people. And somehow, common negativity offers us a sense of comfort. *So is this what it means to be alive?* I think to myself. *Could this be all there is?*

Periodically, the swirl of positive, joyous, and loving thoughts bounce off and out of me. Seeming to be a reflection of life in a different form, the dream of living in this constant state seems too big a desire and dream to be possible. The feelings often seem foreign and look foreign to those around me. The quivering in my belly calls me to stay silent and reflect on what it means to be alive.

Could the birds chirping with joy be an example of aliveness? They seem to sing their own songs, but together they make a wonderful symphony. Could the sound of a river's current, rushing over the rocks, be another example of aliveness? Water is always flowing, sometimes fast, yet other times it looks as if it is standing still. No matter how it looks, it is alive and constantly flowing. The aromas of the flowers bursting with sweetness, oozes into the air. Wow! It tingles my senses. *Are they alive?* Could it be that, despite the variations of flowers that exist, they are simply meant to make people smile? The air that carries their fragrance through the world, while unrecognizable to the sight, exists and is alive. Air creates movement in all existence. Creatures as small as a ladybug and as busy as a chipmunk, move over this planet doing what they were born to do. A butterfly flies, a fish swims, and a snail trudges along as slowly as it desires, but still is moving in its true aliveness.

Be present to appreciate the moment you are in *now*.

Just breathing, doing, and rushing through life is not being alive. It is simply existing. Don't just exist, to where you are numb to the faint scent of the flowers as you rush through the park to get to work. Don't just exist to where you are only stimulated by the artificial noise of rushing cars or loud blaring music in your earbuds. With a disregard for the sight of a passing bird or butterfly, we demonstrate a level of insensitivity or lack of desire to be fully alive.

Being alive beyond existing means that I notice the falling of the leaves as I pass by them. It means that I cannot help myself, but stop and breathe deeply when nature scatters its scents. When I stop to look up to the sky and offer gratitude, I know I am alive. Each moment is once in a lifetime, so I shift into a momentary space of aliveness. Permanent aliveness beyond existing is achieved when I awake each morning with a quiet and calm anticipation for the day. Being alive beyond existing is when my thankful thoughts for the previous day run freely in my mind and I express desire for the day ahead – only to offer loving energy into the world.

Complete and permanent aliveness is a state of being, a beauty that exudes from deep within each of us and out into the world. A life full of magnetizing positivity is a true reflection of aliveness. It exists when you cannot help yourself but smile during a time of outward despair or in the depths of painful seasons – for you can see the beauty in the struggle. When you can only see the good in the world, in others, in situations, and in nature's destructions, you know you are moving toward permanent aliveness.

Turn your sight inward and there you will find the key to your awakening. Awaken to the real life awaiting you. Learn how to live in your aliveness in full splendor. Relish in the tantalizing quivers of being alive beyond existing.

### *Enjoy being alive beyond existing.*

Do you feel alive or that you are just existing every day? Why do you think that is?

What in this world make you feel most alive? Why?

What is one thing you can do that will make you feel more alive?

174

# 78.
# Morning Secrets

O h, how I look forward to the morning.
The early dawn peaks over the horizon and offers warm rays of light. Even just a small flicker of light attempts to stir the world awake. In this morning light exist secrets wanting to be shared.

A cool breeze brushes over nature to usher the creatures to begin their morning routines of stretching, singing, and eating. In harmony with the faint light, the birds begin to chirp. The river flows and reflects more of the dawn's vibrancy upward back into the sky. The fish jump about to begin their feeding before the busyness of the day. The smallest of creatures do not hesitate to wake because they have learned the morning secrets.

As the sun begins to emerge into the full line of sight, its power becomes apparent. It pierces through the greyness to brighten the world. It does not matter if the clouds drift in the sky, the beams of light still poke through, giving positive encouragement for the day ahead.

So, what are the morning secrets?

The secrets are revealed – and I soak up their wisdom – as the sun floats up into its full glory. I have in my reflections that every day is new and a time to start fresh with renewed vigor. Slow is better. When I take it slow each morning and enjoy the peaceful sounds of nature around me, it brings a simple joy to my spirit that lasts throughout the day. It is always possible to shine my light into the world. For, it does not matter how much is seen of my light, just that I shine it bright every day.

Shine bright – you never know when your beam of light will illuminate a path for another.

Every moment is to be cherished. I must not take life for granted. While the sunrise is reliable from dawn to dawn, our awakening is not. Therefore, all life – ours and that of the creatures of the earth – is to be appreciated moment by moment.

So many secrets to share! Let's be captivated and curious about life because every dawn there is a new sound, smell, vision, and creation. I am amazed at the wonders, no matter how simple or complex. Most often the simplest things are the most amazing!

As the sun smiles and gives warmth to the world, so should I each day. It does not take much effort. It is something each of us was created to do. We often get distracted by the darkness in our lives and we forget to smile. We are asked to live in community with one another. As the birds awaken, they flock to one another to say good morning. If they are too far from each other, they share their songs as a way for them to connect. Community is where we get our energy for each day.

Even the simplest secrets are powerful. Breathe. Breathe. Breathe. No matter how hurried the day gets, I must breathe. Intentional breathing simply slows my mind and shifts my focus inward, if only for a second or two. As I learn to slow my morning routine, to appreciate the moments, I end up nourishing myself daily in that quiet time.

Do you take time to nourish yourself each morning? That means taking time to feed your mind, body, and soul with the goodness that they need to survive. The simplest nourishment is water, healthy foods, connection, reflection, nature, fresh air, and sunshine. The sun shines intentionally because it knows we need each other!

*Be a source of love.*

It is simple. The most powerful of the morning secrets is to be love. I must practice this every day without failure. Love simply, like the reliability of the sun rising above the horizon to offer loving rays of warmth throughout the day. As nature offers no judgment every morning, love flows. The birds do not critique other creatures, they simply and lovingly accept the new dawn each day, and proceed to live and love freely. They ask nothing in return. Being love in everything we do, takes great courage, awareness, and intention. While we were created to love out of our nature, the artificial reality that surrounds our moments, distracts each of us into acting artificial.

The morning secrets are shared repeatedly with each dawn because we often forget them throughout the day. Renew the commitment every morning, refresh your perspective on the day ahead, and rejoice in the simplicity of the morning secrets!

### *Rejoice in the new day ahead!*

What is your morning routine? Could you slow it down a bit? If so, how?

What new activities can bring you joy in the morning?

How can you apply some of the morning secrets to your life?

# 79.
# Grateful

Each morning I lie in bed with an inward gaze toward God. I silence the fears, doubts, and negative thoughts in my mind with thoughts of gratitude. It seems to drown out the noise and creates intimacy with Him.

I ask for guidance and direction just for the moment, for the hour, for the day. I ask that my life be used for love, and for purpose. I expect nothing from my requests other than to be present to hear His voice on my heart throughout the day and obey.

I tune my inner compass to service mode each morning. My focus is on how I serve others and Him. By fully utilizing all my giftedness, I am humbly equipped to honor His request of me. It takes a commitment and love of God to recognize one's giftedness and not squander it on self-serving activities each day.

My gratefulness pours through me every hour, and sometimes as it does, tears roll down my face. When moments of blessings are bestowed upon me, I struggle to breathe! I am so overwhelmed by the awesomeness of God, it takes my breath away. My tears are of joy and humble reflection. I smile often in awe struck wonderment of how I am so present in this space at this time. I wasn't always that way. Gratefulness pours through my every thought and keeps my gaze and ear tuned toward Him.

As the day winds down, I reflect on what I accomplished or did not accomplish. I count the smiles, the tears, the hugs, the "thank you" and the "I love you" moments. Some days are just filled with God moments and I am so grateful for the space in my life that allows me to be calm and present to really experience them in such a powerful way.

Other days, I am full of self-indulgent activity so much so that I must recalibrate my thoughts before slumber. I know I was guided throughout the day by Him and He allowed me to wander a bit, so that I could feel the difference of a selfish day versus a servant day.

As I close my eyes, with a grateful heart and quiet my thoughts toward love and vulnerability, I pray for inward remapping of my next step in the journey. Tomorrow is a new refreshing opportunity to shift my thoughts, intensify my focus, and stay deeply committed to serving Him.

The gratitude I feel upon falling asleep each night, and upon awakening each new day, humbles me. I trust and have faith that every step of mine is on purpose, every interaction is to serve and inspire, and every smile emulates love. When I begin to detour, I trust He will put me back on the path of serving Him, not self.

I am so grateful that I have awoken to His daily presence in me! He is my compass as I finish this journey here on earth.

### *Gratitude keeps us humble.*

Who or what is your compass?

What is your gratitude practice?

When is your time for reflection? How can you make it more meaningful?

# 80.
# Sweetness

What do you taste? What do you smell?

In the quietness of a morning walk, the dew coats the body with nourishment. The sound of the ocean waves calls in the peacefulness of the day ahead. The taste of the dew on the tongue is sweet and delicious, just like dawn's promise for our soul. The smell of the salty air mixed with the sweet aroma of the flower blossoms teases all the senses. A calm walk in the forest showers the sweetness on the trees, underfoot, along the side of the trail. Sweetness can be seen, too, in the lusciousness of the blossoms and the vibrancy of colors.

Life is full of sweetness if you are truly alive to taste it. Not just in the morning promises, but the sweetness exists in evening reflective energies. The aliveness of your body's scent on your pillow or on your lover's pillow. How sweet that is! Throughout the day, sweetness of moments that will never repeat themselves again will be forever planted in the memory.

As I started to wake up to life around me and enjoy the moments, life became much sweeter. The simplest pleasure that use to go unnoticed became a treasure for that day. The sweetness would help me endure the painful times,

Enjoy the sweetness of life's little moments. They are decadent, pleasurable, and energize the spirit within. Be present in each experience enough that even the faintest sweetness is tasted and treasured.

### Live a sweet life!

What represents sweetness to you in the morning?

What is your idea of sweetness in the evening?

How can you live more of a sweet life?

# An Invitation to Write

Jacquie Fazekas has a passion for encouraging and inspiring others to live their purpose.

If you would like to consider Jacquie for coaching services, or have her speak to your group, or if you would like to share with Jacquie how *Beyond the Surface* has impacted your life, you can contact her at www.JacquieFazekas.com.

If you enjoyed reading *Beyond the Surface*, Jacquie would appreciate you posting your positive review and comments on her book's purchase page at www.Amazon.com.

Made in the USA
Columbia, SC
21 August 2019